John Cartwright

Take Your Choice!

Representation and Respect, Imposition and Contempt

John Cartwright

Take Your Choice!
Representation and Respect, Imposition and Contempt

ISBN/EAN: 9783744759601

Printed in Europe, USA, Canada, Australia, Japan

Cover: Foto ©Suzi / pixelio.de

More available books at **www.hansebooks.com**

TAKE YOUR CHOICE!

Reprefentation and Refpect:	Impofition and Contempt.

Annual Parliaments and Liberty:	Long Parliaments and Slavery.

Where annual election ends, flavery begins.
                    Hift. Eff. on Brit. Conft.
*A free government, in order to maintain itfelf free, hath need every
    day of fome new provifion in favour of Liberty.*   Machiavel.

*I wifh the maxim of Machiavel was followed, that of examining
    a conftitution, at certain periods, according to its firft principles;
    this would correct abufes and fupply defects.*   Lord Camden.

*And now—in the name of all that is holy—let us confider whether
    a fcheme may not be laid down for obtaining the neceffary re-
    formation of parliament.*   Burgh.

LONDON:

Printed for J. ALMON, oppofite Burlington-Houfe, in
· Piccadilly.

M.DCC.LXXVI.

T O

The Commons of GREAT-BRITAIN,

This Eſſay,

On thoſe Rights and Privileges

Which their Anceſtors thought worth preſerving,

is, with Anxiety and Affection,

inſcribed by

A Fellow Citizen.

October, 1776.

PREFACE.

THE wiseſt men and moſt accompliſhed writers have endeavoured to beſpeak the indulgence of the public by prefaces. A proportionable diffidence in the author of the following ſheets, would wholly conſign them to oblivion; was not that ſentiment over-ruled by a ſenſe of duty, which tells him that he ought to risk every thing, except the reproaches of his own heart, in order to ſerve his country. He believes, that he hath pointed out ſome eſſential conſiderations in the queſtion here diſcuſſed, which have hitherto been overlooked : and that his fellow citizens have been with-held from exerting themſelves, in purſuit of the important object of it, through a perſuaſion that inſuperable difficulties lay in the way. He can aſſure them that no ſuch difficulties exiſt. They have none to contend with, but the ſelfiſhneſs and injuſtice of a ſet of individuals amongſt themſelves, who make only *a three thouſandth part* of their own number. If this ſhall prove an inſuperable difficulty,

he

he shall ceafe to pride himfelf in being
a Briton. That the falvation or the ruin
of his country, depends upon the right
or wrong opinion and conduct of the
commons, with regard to this one fubject,
he thinks will be apparent to every reflecting
man who shall thoroughly confider it. In
this difcuffion, he does not expect that he shall
pleafe either of our two grand national parties; becaufe he flatters neither. His beft
hopes, indeed, are from the *whigs*; becaufe
their creed, *would they but be true to it*, is the
creed of free men: but if *Tories* and *Papifts*
will, in earneft, fet about repairing the conftitution, he will embrace them, and be of
their party. He will, probably, be called an
enthufiaft. He shall not however be shocked
at fuch an appellation; becaufe he believes
that no man, in thefe days, can labour for
the benefit of mankind upon difinterefted
principles, without being reckoned an enthufiaft;—perhaps a Quixote. He will not,
however, be called a flave. Neither shall
any one fay that he is the friend of tyrants.
By fome, he may perhaps be charged with
want of refpect, when he fpeaks of the

Houfe

House of Commons. To them he anfwers; that, towards the conftitutional part of that houfe, no man living bears higher re-fpect than himfelf. He efteems it, he vene-rates, he reveres it. In his eftimation, there is more honour and dignity in fitting there the real reprefentative of two or three thoufand free men, and the immediate guardians of public liberty; than having place amongft nobles, or being feated on an hereditary throne itfelf. But, if there be any part of that houfe which is not conftitutional, he fcruples not to acknowledge, that it moves, and ever will move, his indignation and contempt, and excite his abhorrence. And he knows of no obligation which a Briton is under, not to ex-pofe and condemn any thing whatever in the legiflature of his country, which is a palpable departure from the conftitution, and threaten-ing to public freedom. With regard to the Houfe of Commons, he would facrifice a great deal, to be able to prove his own words a libel. He pretends not to write to philofo-phers and men of letters, fo much as to his fellow citizens at large. For the former, the abftract elements of parliamentary fcience would

would be sufficient; and might be contained in three pages. But a more argumentative and explanatory manner, a plainer and indeed a coarser language is necessary for the unrefined, though sensible, bulk of the people. 'Tis them he wishes to inform, to move, to direct, towards the security of their liberties; which he apprehends to be in danger. Let his work, then, be considered in that light; and, if esteemed a necessary one which better writers have neglected, let it be read with candour, and meet with the indulgence due to an useful, though in-elegant performance.

INTRODUCTION.

HAVING propofed to urge upon you, my countrymen! a reformation, both as to the length, and as to the conftituting of your parliaments; it feems but proper, previoufly to ftate fome of the inconveniencies and evils, which I apprehend to be the neceffary confequences of, and infeparable from, our prefent rotten parliamentary fyftem.

All men will grant, that the lower houfe of parliament is elected by only a handful of the commons, inftead of the whole; and this, chiefly by bribery and undue influence. Men who will employ fuch means are villains; and thofe who dupe their conftituents by lying promifes, are far from honeft men. An affembly of fuch men is *founded* on *iniquity:* confequently, the fountain of legiflation is poifoned. Every ftream, how much foever mixed, as it flows with juftice and patriotifm, will ftill have poifon in its compofition.

Nor will it be denied me, that, in confequence of the long duration of a parliament, the members, as foon as feated, feel themfelves too independent on the opinion and good will of their conftituents, even where their fuffrages have not been extorted nor bought; and that, of courfe, they defpife them.

From the firft of thefe data, it will follow, that we are fubject to have the Houfe of

B   Com-

Commons filled by men of every bad defcription that can be thought of, and that ftrict
integrity, which ought to be the ftrongeft of
all recommendations, amounts to a pofitive
exclufion; except it happen indeed to be
be united with a capital fortune and great
county connections.

From the firft and fecond jointly; our reprefentatives, who are in fact our deputed
fervants, are taught to affume the carriage
and haughtinefs of defpotic mafters; to think
themfelves unaccountable for their conduct;
and to neglect their duty.

Whether, indeed, the houfe of commons be in a great meafure filled with
idle fchool-boys, infignificant coxcombs,
led-captains and toad-eaters, profligates, gamblers, bankrupts, beggars, contractors, com-
miffaries, public plunderers, minifterial de-
pendants, hirelings, and wretches, that would
fell their country, or deny their God for a
guinea, let every one judge for himfelf.
And whether the kind of bufinefs very often
brought before the houfe, and the ufual
manner of conducting it, do not befpeak
this to be the cafe; I likewife leave every
man to form his own opinion: particularly
that independent and noble-minded few, who
experience the conftant mortification of voting
and fpeaking without even a hope of being
able thereby to ferve their country.

But

But without infifting on thefe things as fact, and only admitting the poffibility of them from the combined caufes already affigned, of long parliaments, undue influence and bribery, it is natural to expect, as indeed all experience fhews it muft happen, that a country, whofe affairs are *fubject to fall* into fuch hands muft be ruined, fooner or later, by thofe very men who fhall be in the office of its guardians and prefervers; except it fhall make an alteration in this particular.

And accordingly, we find our own country in a condition which fhews that its affairs have long been in fuch hands. It has paffed through all the ftages of abufe, and is at length arrived at a precipice tremendous to look from. The current of corruption is fmooth and flattering; and it meanders for a while through fcenes not unpleafant to the carelefs paffengers: but it is deceitful, and fure to terminate in a Niagarian fall; and to dafh its navigators headlong into the abyfs of flavery and wretchednefs, unlefs they take warning in time and will manfully exert themfelves. Our giddy veffel of ftate is fwiftly gliding down this current; and, by the velocity with which the paffing fhores of our fair provinces fly from our wondering eyes and are loft to fight, we may know that we are in the dreadful vortex, and we may hear the very roaring of the cataract. But yet, we need not perifh, except the character of our

nation

nation hath forfaken us. The Englifh failor, whether naval or political, is imprudent and thoughtlefs enough, God knows; but when dangers furround him, or an enemy comes in fight, he fhews that he is neither a coward nor a lubber; he knows how to deal with either of them. We fhould, on this occafion do no more than right, were we to begin our work with putting the law of *Oleron* in execution, by throwing overboard our befotted pilots: not but that I think, there will be more magnanimity in fuffering even thofe wretches to fhare in the general prefervation.

But, dropping thefe metaphors, let us proceed with the propofed detail of the moft material public inconveniencies and evils which may be attributed to the ufage of long parliaments.

I. The kingdom, under long (and always meaning corrupt) parliaments, hath been proverbial for making war without wifdom, and peace without policy. And yet, one of the pretences againft annual parliaments hath been, that they would occafion fuch minifterial inftability and incertitude of national councils, that foreign powers would not confide in your treaties nor alliances. But this, fo far as *we* have any bufinefs with the argument, is diametrically oppofite to the truth. Annual parliaments will always adhere to the true interefts of the nation; and upon all
alliances

alliances formed upon that bafis, foreigners would moft affuredly rely, fooner than upon the faith of kings. But annual parliaments would not, it is true, fuffer minifters to ne-gociate away the blood and treafure of this kingdom, in order to flatter the weakneffes or partialities of the prince, nor to gratify their own avarice or ambition. Such parliaments would, moreover, give ftability and perma-nency to adminiftrations; by extinguifhing party and faction, and leaving a minifter of ftate nothing to do but to attend to the duties of his office and the preparing of plans for the public good. He would no longer have the greateft part of his time taken up in, forming and conducting one 'faction, and oppofing the reft; nor would his ftation then have thofe charms for an unprincipled man which it has at prefent. It would only be de-firable to men of a generous ambition for ferv-ing their country by their perfonal labours, and who could content themfelves with no more power than fhould be confiftent with the liberties of their fellow citizens. Such men would be too eftimable in the opinion of the public, and confequently in the judg-ment of an annual parliament, ever to be difturbed with an ill-intended oppofition to their wife and honeft meafures. Oppofi-tion, from which alone we find protection againft tyranny in the prefent corrupt ftate of things, is in itfelf an evil : but one that would vanifh

vanifh together with long parliaments; for to them it owes its being, and with them muſt die. An annual parliament properly chofen, would not be compofed of two or three contending factions, each aiming at power by the overthrow of its rivals; but would be in fact, as in theory it is called, a national council. The opinion of every individual (making fome allowances for oratory) would have its weight, in proportion to its folidity: and it would be the defire of a very great majority of the members to affift the minifter in perfecting his plans of government by fage advice; not to oppofe nor to fupport, right or wrong, according to pay or party.

II. It has been owing to the conftant facrifices which have been made of the national interefts to the feparate interefts of the court, that fo many continental connections and fubfidiary engagements have been formed by our minifters under the fanction of long parliaments. Befides the lavifh wafte of money which have been occafioned, the demands upon us for troops, have brought us to imagine a very confiderable army neceffary to us. Hence in a great meafure it is, that our military eftablifhment is fo large, and fo kept up, as to be but half a ftep from a ftanding army in the worft fenfe of thofe words.

III. And it has been in order to anfwer minifterial, not national purpofes, that an army has been kept in our colonies during peace,

peace. So far from their being for the protection of the colonies againſt the irruptions
of the ſavages, the troops never were ſeen
upon the borders; but were quartered in the
chief towns along the ſea coaſt, for the tyrannical purpoſe of keeping the people in awe.

IV. Our country, fertile as it is by nature,
enriched by commerce, and inhabited by
a people characteriſtically active and induſ-
trious, is neverthelefs mortgaged like the
eſtate of a prodigal. We groan under the
burthen of an enormous debt; no lefs than
137 millions ſterling : while our miniſters are
ſtill going on in the ways of waſte and pro-
fuſion. This debt is not only a grievous evil
in itſelf; but it is a fruitful parent of other
evils. Amongſt the moſt conſiderable, are
its making ſo many people creatures of the
crown, by being dependent for a livelihood
on the manifold arrangements reſpecting our
funds. Hereby a very powerful and united
party is formed againſt every reformation in
finance. Money'd property in the funds alſo
converts whole herds of men into drones, who
contribute nothing towards the public ſtock;
but, on the contrary, are a dead weight on
the induſtry of the nation.

Under annual parliaments (always ſup-
poſing them to have contained a full repre-
ſentation of the commons) theſe evils would
not have been known : or if any temporary
debt

debt had been unavoidably contracted, it would as certainly have been speedily discharged. The nation would consequently be in no danger of bankruptcy from any untoward event, as it is at present; and would have been at all times ready to repel the attacks of its enemies. But the *feelings* of the great bulk of the *nation*, are not the same with the *feelings* of *long parliaments* founded in corruption: nor will the *language* of such parliaments to their prince, ever express *the sense of the people*.

V. Are not our sanguinary statutes, by which we year by year spill rivers of blood, a reproach to the political knowledge, to the humanity, to the religion of our island? And are not our prisons and our treatment of prisoners shocking and foolish?

VI. Are we not suffering from the distress and idleness of the poor, and from a visible depopulation; and do we not leave millions of acres uncultivated?

VII. Is not the metropolis and the whole kingdom over-run with vagrants and beggars, notwithstanding our astonishing provisions against want?

VIII. Is not every city, town and village, crowded with alehouses, those hotbeds of idleness and vice? And are not gaming and adultery, amongst the higher ranks of the people, become such enormities in a civilized com-

community, as to cry aloud for the attention
of the legiflature ? *

IX. Are we not alienating the affections
of the people from the crown by injuries and
infult. ?. Are we not grieving and provoking
peaceable fubjects, and thereby nourifhing
fects and fchifms by adhering to their detriment to trifles and to nonfenfe in church
government; inftead of facrificing them to
good fenfe and charity, and forming a new
pale for our church on the foundations of
reafon and truth ?

But when will any national evil ever be
taken into confideration, and corrected by
the *fpontaneous* act of a long parliament ?
Men who are too ignorant to legiflate for
a tavern club, or who are voluptuaries and
debauchees, or whofe whole thoughts are en-
groffed by the loaves and filhes, are they

---

* When I had fed them to the full, they then committed adultery, and affembled themfelves by troops
in the harlots houfes. They were as fed horfes in the
morning ; every one neighed after his neighbour's wife.
Shall I not vifit for thefe things ? faith the Lord : and
fhall not my foul be avenged on fuch a nation as this ?
Jeremiah, c. 5; which is entitled, The judgments of God
upon the *Jews* for their *manifold corruptions.* But we are
Chriftians; and it hath moreover pleafed the Lord, to raife
up the Earl of Chefterfield (fee his letter Dec. 3, 1763)
in thefe our days, to declare it in the houfe of Jacob and
publifh it in Judah, that *adultery* (fee feveral of his letters)
and *treafon to our country*, (fee vol. II. let. 161) are amongft
the virtues of a fenator, and the proper pleafures of a man
of fafhion.

to

to watch over the good of a great nation, to remark its deviations into political error, and to recal it by wife inftitutions? Is it not known by too melancholy an experience, that the propofer of any individual improvement, is firft received with the coldnefs of a mifer to a beggar of alms; and if his zeal for the public be too ftrong to be damped by fuch ufage, that he is then oppofed and baited in parliament as a mad enthufiaft? Who can tell me of any the leaft improvement in our laws and policy that hath been made of late years by long parliaments, which has not been the fole effect of fome very fpirited exertion in individuals, favoured by the circumftances of the day, and backed by fome preffing and urgent evil which could no longer be endured? What fort of an idea does this give one of *a national council?* 10, 100, 1000, 10,000. But to recite, one by one, the evils proceeding from long parliaments, would require volumes. And it is to be noted that there is not a public evil exifting, which would have been prevented or would now be remedied by an annual, that ought not to be placed to the account of a long parliament. The reader, if he wifhes to go deep into that enquiry, will do well to perufe the political difquifitions of the late Mr. Burgh. I will only further fay in general, that, to the extreme venality of the boroughs and the proftitution in parliament, to the barefaced

pillage

pillage of the public treasure practised by minifters, and their prefering men without the
fmalleft regard to decency in point of character, are originally owing without doubt,
that fordid devotion to avarice which hath
generally infected the people from the higheft
to the loweft, and that almoft univerfal in-
fenfibility to the public good which accom-
panies it. Inftead of counteracting the natural ill effects of luxury proceeding from
wealth and profperity, and giving it a beneficial
turn by wife and humane laws; it has been
the bufinefs of *government* (which " in almoft
every age and country," fays Burgh " has
been the principal *grievance* of the people")
to debauch and corrupt the manners and
morals of the people, by every poffible inven-
tion; in order to remove every obftacle in the
way to abfolute power. It beats up and bids
high for volunteers in iniquity. The greater
felons, who are ready at its command to
deftroy their country, are careffed and re-
warded: but little ones, indeed, who take
a purfe or fteal a fheep, are hanged without
remorfe, for not being proof againft example
and temptation. Is not every man taught to
fell himfelf, his honour, his confcience, his
foul, for a price! And is not he who hath a
fcruple, the butt of minifterial ridicule! We
fhould juftly efteem that mariner mad, who,
in order to carry a leaky fhip to the end of a
long voyage, fhould be continually boring

C 2   frefh

frefh holes in her bottom. Is there lefs mad-
nefs in corrupting the parliament, in order to
carry on the bufinefs of government? He
who knows no better mode of governing than
that, is fit to govern no where but in the
infernal regions.

This has been more or lefs the condition of
our government ever fince we have had long
parliaments. " We fee the fame corrupt or
" impolitic proceedings going on in the ad-
" miniftration of a *Harley*, a *Walpole*, a *Pel-*
" *ham*, a *Pitt*, a *Bute*, a *Grafton*, a *North*;
" and we fee every parliament implicitly obey-
" ing the orders of the minifter. Some mi-
" nifters we fee more criminal, others lefs;
" fome parliament more flavifh, others lefs';
" but we fee all minifters and all parliaments,
" *the prefent always excepted*, guilty; in-
" excufably guilty, in fuffering the continual
" and increafing prevalency of corruption,
" from miniftry to miniftry, and from parlia-
" ment to parliament.[a]" But there never has
been a time when thefe defcriptions were fo
applicable as they are at prefent. Are not
men of the moft blafted characters the con-
fidential fervants of the crown? Are not the
fcales of council weighed down with minifterial ayes and noes inftead of folid and
weighty arguments; and is not all parliamentary debate become a mockery? Have not
millions of your unoffending brethren in Ame-

[a] Pol. Difq. vol. III. p. 452.

rica

rica been devoted by mercenary majorities to
flavery or to flaughter? Is not your commerce put to the hazard on a caft, whether
or not it fhall be ruined? And are you not
inviting an unequal war; all to no one end
or purpofe, but becaufe two or three def-
perate ideots will have it fo, rather than
abandon the vicious fchemes of ambition they
had once formed? Have not defaulters of
millions upon millions conftantly efcaped
parliamentary vengeance! And fiends who
have fattened on the famine and butchery
of the inoffenfive *Afiatics*, are they not
amongft your legiflators, refpected and ho-
noured!—What national depravity, what ex-
tremes of wickednefs, and what public cala-
mities muft we not experience, while the
fountain of legiflation and the fprings of
government are fo impure!—

So ruinous a fyftem needs muft, in its
progrefs, grow worfe and worfe. The cha-
riot of corruption, (if I may be allowed a
new metaphor) under the guidance of rotten
whigs would foon enough have arrived, without the whip, at the goal of defpotifm: but
now, that furious tories have feized the
reins, 'tis lafhed onward with impetuous
hafte; nor do they feem fenfible to their
danger, though its axles are already on fire
with its rapidity. The minifters of the prefent reign have daringly ftruck at your moft
facred rights, have aimed through the fides

of

óf America a deadly blow at the life of your conftitution, and have ſhewn themſelves hoſtile, not only to the being, but to the very name of liberty. The word itſelf has been proſcribed the court; and for any one who dared to utter it, the gentleft appella‑ tions have been Wilkite, republican and diſ‑ turber of the peace. Facts recent in every one's memory I have no need to repeat. I will only therefore juſt mention the atrocious violation of the firſt principle of the conſtitu‑ tion in the never-to-be forgotten buſineſs of the Middleſex election. An enumeration of all their crimes would ſhew them to be de‑ ſerving of the higheſt puniſhments. And yet, the ſum of all the evils they have brought upon us, added to all thoſe which former miniſters had intailed upon the nation, are light and trivial in compariſon of the one great evil of a long parliament. Feaſt the fowls of the air with ſuch miniſters, but leave your legiſlature unreformed; and you will only add a few inglorious days to the pe‑ riod of your expiring liberties. Succeeding miniſters might be more circumſpect; but, with the aid of a proſtitute parliament, they would at length ſucceed. " Could we have " had every one of our corrupt miniſters im‑ " peached, and even convicted, would a cor‑ " rupt parliament filled with their obſequious " tools, have puniſhed them ? If we did no‑ " thing

" thing toward a radical cure of grievances,
" and obliging the fucceeding to be honefter
" than the foregoing; what fhould we have
" gained by fuch profecutions? The greateft
" part of the *Roman* emperors was maffacred,
" and fo are many of *Afiatic* and *African* ty-
" rants, But did the *Romans* or do the *Turks*,
" and the people of *Algiers*, gain any ad-
" ditional liberty by the punifhment of their
" oppreffors? We know they did not. Nor
" fhall we by clamouring, nor even by
" punifhing; any more than we ftop rob-
" bing on the highway by hanging, un-
" lefs we put it out of the *power* of minifters
" to go on abufing us and trampling upon our
" liberties; and this can only be done by re-
" ftoring independency to parliament ᵇ." It
is downright quixotifm to imagine, that fo
long as your parliament remains corrupt, you
can ever have a patriot minifter: and, except
parliament be reformed, 'tis a matter of very
great indifference who are *in* and who are *out*.
I will not utterly deny the poffibility of your
having a patriot minifter prior to a parliamentary reformation; but I do not myfelf conceive
how fuch a man is to arrive at fuch a ftation.
One of that ftamp could not go through thick
and thin, and wade through all the miry paths
that lead to it: nor have I any great expecta-
tion of a miraculous converfion of any one,
who hath once paffed through thofe ways to

ᵇ Pol. Difq. vol. III. p. 452.

the

the feat of power. Neither do I fee the prudence of waiting for fo rare a phenomenon as
a patriot minifter, to do that for you which
you can do for yourfelves; and thereby put
things in fuch a ftate, that a patriot minifter
will no longer be a phenomenon, but a natural and common appearance.

The revolution which expelled the tyrant
James from the throne, glorious as it was to
the character, and effential to the fafety of this
nation, was yet a very defective proceeding.
It was effected in too anxious a moment, and
in too precipitate a manner, to lay a lafting
foundation for the fecurity of public freedom
and profperity. *William* the deliverer was
but half the friend to liberty which he pretended to be. Had he been a truly patriot
prince, his fhare in the expulfion of a tyrant
would have been his fmalleft merit; and he
would have embraced the opportunity afforded
him by his own fuccefs and the tide of reformation being fet in, to have guarded the
conftitution againft every conceivable danger
towards which it had any tendency to be ex-
pofed in procefs of time. When the im-
mortal and bleffed *Alfred* had overthrown the
oppreffors of his country, he thought the
work of a king only begun; and devoted the
reft of his reign to the correcting abufes,
the eftablifhing of juftice, and laying the
broad foundations of liberty and happinefs.

nefs [c]. But hiftory fhews *William* to have
been a cold-hearted Dutchman, ungrateful to
a people who had given him a crown, and
more fond of power than of fquaring his government with the principles of the conftitution. And this was one of the beft of
our kings. Then put not your truft in
princes: neither have confidence in minifters!
Whether they covet inordinate power for its
own fake, or for the fake of lucre, they will
have it if poffible. And when one lufts for
gold, the other for dominion, they will be
reciprocally the pimps to each others paffion.
The prince will invade the people's property,
in order to enrich his minifter; the minifter
will violate their liberties, in order to render
his mafter abfolute. For one *Alfred*, there
are a thoufand *Charles's*; for one *Falk-
land*, a thoufand *Walpoles*. Truft not, I
fay, in princes nor in minifters; but truft in
ÿourfelves, and in reprefentatives chofen
by yourfelves alone!

[c] " It is delivered down to us as a proof of the good
" government of king *Alfred*; that a maiden bearing
" a purfe of money in her hand might in his reign have
" gone from one end of the kingdom to the other, without
" fear of violence either to her perfon or property. How
" is it with us ? Can a man almoft fleep in his bed within
" the walls of our metropolis; &c." *Further Examination*,
p. 142.

TAKE

TAKE YOUR CHOICE!

HEREDITARY
ELEVATION
REPRESENTATION
EQUAL
& ANNUAL

NATURAL
AND
CIVIL LIBERTY

UNANIMITY MILITIA AND NAVY

It is this extending & contracting proportion that adds
stability to any government &c
Blackstones Com. Vol. 1. p. 156

GREAT THEATRE ROYAL

ARMY

REGAL PROPERTY

When a building is completed the scaffolding
may be thrown down

Publish'd by I. Almon in Piccadilly, Oct.14: 1776 as the Act Directs.

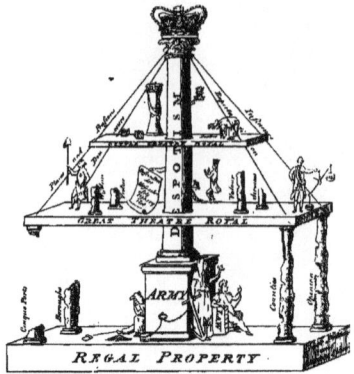

TAKE YOUR CHOICE!

SECTION I.

THE human fpecies form an intermediate clafs, between the angelick and irrational orders of exiftence. They are intended for a fphere of action and a degree of happinefs, in a future ftate, of which their prefent faculties can give them no accurate conception: but thefe only on condition of their having acted virtuoufly in this life; which their Creator has told them is no more than a ftate of probation. The firft, and great end, then, of their exiftence, is, by the ftudy of wifdom and practice of virtue, to be conftantly approximating towards moral perfection; in order to the attainment of that future exaltation and happinefs: and the next material, and indeed only remaining point, is, to render themfelves, individually and collectively, as happy as poffible during their term of mor-

D 2   tality;

tality; to which they are alfo invited by the whole law of nature and religion. They have, therefore, neceffarily been created free. Were it otherwife, neither virtue nor vice, right nor wrong, could be afcribed to their actions; and to talk of happinefs, would be to talk nonfenfe.

Hence, they are doubtlefs under an eternal obligation to preferve their freedom to the utmoft of their power : becaufe, by parting with it, in *any degree* more or lefs, they *fo far* deprive themfelves of the means of doing their duty, and of performing thofe actions which the laws of virtue may require of them; and becaufe, they will thereby make themfelves, and frequently their pofterity, fubfervient alfo to the wicked defigns of thofe, to whofe power they have fubmitted. That people, who have fuffered their prince to become a tyrant over themfelves, foon find themfelves employed as the inftruments of his lawlefs will, in extending the limits of tyranny, and fpreading devaftation amongft their fellow creatures. How bafe and degrading is fuch a condition!

2. The all-wife creator hath likewife made men by nature equal, as well as free. They are all of " one flefh," and caft in one mould. There are given to them the fame fenfes, feelings and affections, to inform and to influence; the fame paffions to actuate;
the

the fame reafon to guide; the fame moral principle to reftrain; and the fame free will to determine, all alike.

There are, therefore, no diftinctions to be made amongft men, as juft caufes for the elevation of fome above the reft, prior to *mutual agreement*. How much foever any individual may *be qualified for or deferve* any elevation, he hath no *right* to it, till it be conferred upon him by his fellows. There is perhaps, more occafion to advert to this diftinction between *defert of authority*, and a *right to authority*, obvious as it is, than may be commonly imagined. As *all* elevation depends upon common confent; fo it may, confequently, whenever found inconfiftent with the common good, be, by common confent, abolifhed.

Hence we find that it is liberty, not dominion, which is held by *divine* right. The prince as a *man* has, in common with other men, a divine right of being exempt from any unneceffary reftraints; but, as a *king*, all his rights are derived from the *common confent of the people*, of whom he made, prior to his elevation, an individual only equal with the reft. His portion of the fovereign power of the ftate is greater by many degrees than any other man's; but ftill it is only a *portion*, and every man in the community is, in a fmaller degree, *a joint partaker with him* in the fovereign power. If it be the poffeffion of fupreme power in ftates which

which conftitutes kings, then are a free people a nation of kings; for every man, where
there is freedom, has a fhare in the fupreme
power.

3. An accidental fuperiority in mufcular
ftrength or perfonal accomplifhments; that
finenefs of organization and harmony of phy-
fical caufes from which proceed clearnefs of
intellect, parts and genius; that cultivation
of the mind which produces knowledge and
wifdom; but, more efpecially, that rectitude
of the heart which conftitutes virtue; are all
juft caufes of diftinction in fociety; and have
accordingly raifed men in all ages and coun-
tries to an elevation above their fellow citizens,
by common confent. And it is to be noted,
that, in no age or country hath *common confent*
ever elevated particular men above their fellows, for either their vices, follies or infirmities [d]; or for any other reafons, but in
order to promote the common good, or to
exprefs the public gratitude for good already
received. But *kings* and *minifters* do often
elevate thofe very men, who would be the
laft to whom their fellow citizens would fhew
fuch a preference.

4. In fmall communities only, fuited to democratical government in its purity, have all

---

[d] The fuperftitions and grofs prejudices of *idolatrous*
and *barbarous* nations, may have led them into fuch ab-
furdities: but that, it is prefumed, will not form any
folid objection to the juftnefs of this remark.

diſtinctions been made in favour of merit;
and in ſuch alone hath it, therefore, been
ever poſſible for the elevation of particular
perſons above the reſt, to operate, in its full
effect for the common weal.

5. But, in larger communities, where this
pure democratical or republican form of government cannot be carried into practice, it
hath been found expedient to make *artificial*,
as well as natural diſtinctions amongſt men;
and even to agree upon *hereditary* elevations.
And, notwithſtanding there is herein a departure from ſtrict natural juſtice; and that,
by ſuch means, hereditary virtue is ſo far
from being inſured, that ſuch an elevation in-
creaſes the difficulties of being virtuous, in
thoſe who are born to it; yet, theſe artificial
and hereditary elevations have, nevertheleſs,
under judicious regulations, been found by experience, to anſwer very great and good purpoſes to large ſtates. The nature of the caſe,
however, makes it apparent, that the powers
annexed to all ſuch elevations, which are altogether as we have obſerved an infringement
on rigid juſtice, ought to be circumſcribed by
very clear and *impaſſable* limitations, and ulti-
mately to depend on the will of the people;
for whoſe benefit and ſecurity theſe elevations
have been, or ought to have been contrived.
Nay, ſo far as we have either light or authority
to pronounce, the great rule and end of every
divine inſtitution which concerns mankind, has
been

bcen the benefit of *the species at large*; and not the elevation of *particular persons*. There have been men, however, even *Englishmen*, who have written books, in order to prove that persons neither wiser nor better, but oftentimes more worthless and despicable than other men, have been elevated for *their own sakes*; and that drivelers and scoundrels have had a *divine* right to be the guardians, the guides and lawgivers of mankind. I am myself inclined to believe that the Deity is no respecter of persons. It being a fundamental maxim of the English constitution, that the title and authority of a *king* depends upon common consent, or the will of the people; it will, I conceive, necessarily follow that *all inferior* titles and authority, which flow from, and are as it were included in, the regal office, must lie under the same predicament. And indeed we have frequently asserted this doctrine by acts of attainder; whereby peerages with all their privileges have been abolished. Not to mention that, with regard to Roman catholics, this power of the people, though mitigated, is constantly in a state of exertion. Though not divested of their titles, they are deprived of their parliamentary authority and privileges. Seeing, then, that all elevations depend on the will of the people, and that common consent never causes *unnecessary* elevations, nor elevates *unworthy* objects; we may see how much it is the duty of a king, to

whom

whom this important power is delegated, to
confult, in all the elevations he makes, the
good and the *pleafure* of the people alone.
Should he raife men by wholefale to the houfe
of peers, for no other caufe than their fervility to the court while in the houfe of commons, he would doublefs betray his truft;
and it would be high time to form an *impaffa-
ble* limitation, beyond which the numbers of
the peers fhould never extend. A more numerous peerage than fhould give refpect and
dignity to that order of men, than fhould form
a well proportioned council of ftate and court
of judicature, and conftitute a due balancing
power between the king and the commons,
fhould never be exceeded. An excefs muft
neceffarily operate againft the good of the
public.

6. When we reflect upon the nature of
thofe artificial and hereditary elevations which
obtain in the complicated frames of mixed
governments like our own; and duly confider
their *ufual* caufes, and their attendant circumftances; together with their too common
effects upon the frailty of human nature;
when, I fay, we thus deeply reflect, it becomes apparent to reafon, and it is abundantly
proved by experience, that it is utterly unfafe
for the *commons* of any community, to intruft
in the hands of the few who are thus *fet apart* by
hereditary, or *detached* in any degree from the
common intereft by artificial, elevations, any

E   of

of thofe powers on which more immediately depend the prefervation of their liberties. Amongft thefe, the powers of the purfe have the firft place. So fure as the *few* fhall ever obtain the power of taxing, at their difcretion, the *many*; fo fure will the latter be in a ftate of fervitude. It is therefore, on the foundeft principles of wifdom, that the commons of this kingdom are fcrupuloufly tenacious of the powers of the public purfe; and exercife the exclufive right of originating, and wholly modelling, every parliamentary act which fhall operate in the nature of a tax. When they fhall ceafe to do this, they will ceafe to be free.

7. The legiflative powers of our conftitution have been intrufted in the hands of a king, nobles, and a limited number of delegates, to be nominated by, and to reprefent the *commons*; or that part of the people *which remains*, after the king and the nobles have been fet apart ᵉ. Pains have alfo been taken

---

ᵉ The neglect of this neceffary diftinction has in various excellent writers, occafioned obfcurity. And others have *purpofely* neglected it, in order to confound. " It is not;" fays a moft elegant an honeft writer, " the " three eftates, but thofe whom the *people* elect, who re " prefent them." Here, he doubtlefs fhould have faid *commons*. *Appeal to the juftice and interefts of the people of Great Britain in the prefent difputes with America.* " In a free ftate, every man, who is fuppofed a free agent, " ought to be, in fome meafure, his own governor; and " therefore a *branch* at leaft of the legiflative power fhould " refide

to effect a due poize of the feveral members of this legiflative body, and to define the diftinct duties and privileges of each; fo that both its feparate movements, and its joint operations fhall be fuch, as beft to bring about thofe ends for which it was inftituted: namely, the fecurity, profperity and happinefs of the whole.

8. It is confeffed by foreigners and boafted by Englifhmen, that our conftitution of government is the beft that hath ever yet been framed by human wifdom. Moft of the caufes which contribute towards this very fuperior excellence, are obvious to but flight obfervers: but, if I miftake not, there is one particular caufe, perceived only by the more contemplative, to which it is owing in a fuper-eminent degree. I mean that perfect harmony and correfpondence which our con-ftitution of government, in its *genuine fpirit and purity*, holds with the great conftitution of moral government, called the law of na-

---

" refide in the whole body of the *people*." Here again it fhould have been *commons*. *Black. Com.* Vol. I. p. 158.

" Surely the nation might have expelled Mr. Wilkes,
" or have ftruck his name out of the lift of committee,
" had it been affembled, and had it thought proper fo to do.
" What then fhould hinder the *deputies of the nation* from
" doing the fame thing?" Here *nation* is fynonymous with *people*. It is firft ufed properly, and afterwards it artfully calls the *commons* by the fame name. The houfe of com-mons are not the deputies of the *nation* or *people*, but the deputies of the *commons* only. *Tucker's Tracts*, p. 172.

ture.

ture. The excellence of our common law cannot be more ftrongly expreffed, than by its well-known definition, of being " the per-fection of human reafon. The conftitution is a frame of government co-eval with, erected upon, and regulated by, the fpirit of the common law of England. It may confe-quently be defined to be a government agree-able to the perfection of human reafon." The *uncertainty* of our common law is, not-withftanding the ludicrous ufe often made of thofe words, truly *glorious*. Departing from former precedents and decifions which are any way defective, in order to come nearer and, nearer to the perfection of human reafon, its determinations continue to vary and to refine, as experience and wifdom dictate. When the perfection of reafon, on any point, is once attained; then, and not till then, is our law *unalterable*[f]. And until the like per-fection, on any point refpecting the frame of our government, be arrived at; the like glorious uncertainty belongs to the Englifh conftitution. But this uncertainty in the conftitution we have no reafon to be alarmed at; becaufe it can only operate to its im-provement, as the other does to the amend-ment of the law. Nay, it is the duty of our

---

[f] An alteration muft be for the *worfe* and therefore *wrong*: and it is abfurd to fuppofe that any legiflature can have a *right* to do *wrong*.

legiflators

legiflators to declare and to vindicate this uncertainty; and, from time to time, to amend
by it our frame of government; which, tho'
" *agreeable to* the perfection of human reafon,"
is but, as yet, in a ftate of approximation
towards that abfolute ideal perfection we very
properly attribute to it ᵉ. This, I fay, is
the duty of our legiflators, as much as it is
the duty of our judges to depart from all
defective precedents in law decifions, and to
eftablifh new ones in their room, more agreeable to truth and right reafon. And this improvement of the conftitution ought at all
times to be made, were it only fuggefted by
reafon, and not by inconveniences and miferies
already felt. A dog, a horfe, or an afs will grow
wife by *experience*, and learn to fhun what has
injured him. And, if, inftead of making
improvements, any grofs abufes, or a perver-
fion of the cleareft principles of the conftitution were to be practifed by thefe legiflators,
to the detriment of the people; it would be
a language far too mild and forbearing to fay
only that they *neglected* their duty. But,
fhould we ever obferve them, feduloufly to
feek out all thofe points on which no conftitutional doctrine had yet been enacted into
pofitive law, and there to make their attacks;

ᵉ Kingftone caufe : in which has been over-ruled a defective mode of adminiftering juftice, that had been practifed 1475 years.

in

in order to deftroy the conftitution itfelf, and
in its ftead to render themfelves the arbiters of
our lives and liberties, would it not be time
to act a little for ourfelves, inftead of con-
tinuing wholly to confide in fuch treacherous
agents? We ought at leaft to act the part of
a diftruftful mafter; by requiring them, on
the points in queftion, to make the written
law fpeak the true language of the conftitution: and this we ought to do in fuch a tone,
as to convince them that we meant to have
our commands punctually obeyed.

9. Whenever we may think fuch a conduct
neceffary, and fhall ferioufly take up the
matter, thefe verfatile gentlemen will affect
to applaud the rectitude of our intentions;
but at the fame time, they will not be wanting in their kind endeavours, to fhew us that
we are ignorant of the fubject, and have mis-
judged the meafures proper for the occafion.
They will, with all imaginary dexterity,
fhift off, if poffible, all fufpicion of blame
from themfelves; and, by an inundation of
words to overwhelm the truth, and by the
fubtileft arts, to warp the judgment, they
will hope to fatisfy us that the grofs corruption and misgovernment we have complained of, were mere creatures of the ima-
gination. Whatever may happen to be too
glaring to be hid by any veil, and they fhall
condefcendingly acknowledge to be wrong in
itfelf, they will take efpecial care to juftify,

or at leaft extenuate, by a *neceffity* arifing from
the licentioufnefs of the people: and, as far
as they fhall dare, they will infinuate that
the cure of this licentioufnefs, and confequently of the evils complained of, would be,
to arm the crown or themfelves with greater
and more fummary powers. If all thefe admirable arguments fhould fail them, they
would then be feized with fad apprehenfions
and horrors at the thoughts of *innovations*.
Every intended improvement of the conftitution, and even the reftoration of any former
falutary practices, would all be, in their artful language, dangerous innovations; and
there would be no end of their declamation.
Happily for us they have no prefcriptive title
to infallibility; and therefore they cannot,
like his Holinefs, abfolutely forbid us the ufe
of our reafon in matters of government.
They will, however, on fuch an occafion, like
all other benevolent impoftors their pre-
deceffors, do all they can to work on the prejudices of the people, or rather the commons;
and to perfuade them that things are mighty
fafe if they would but think fo; but that,
fhould they unwifely either remove, or re-
ftrict, fuch faithful and able fervants, their
affairs muft all go to wreck and ruin.

10. Here, I confefs, I am afraid of their
abilities, and that their arts will meet with too
much fuccefs. Let the friends of freedom,
then, guard againft their artifices, and take

care

care to blunt thofe weapons with which it is known they will attempt to wound ftill deeper their bleeding country. With this view, our fellow citizens fhould be perpetually warned on this delicate point; and taught how to diftinguifh between what are, and what are not, innovations; as well as between innovations which may be dangerous, and innovations which might be eligible. *See Polit. Difq.* vol. 3. p. 298, 303, 304.

11. Changes and alterations in government which fhould proceed from caprice, ficklenefs, or a mere fpirit of innovating, without any *fixed ftandard* or *fure criterion*, by which they were to be regulated and might be judged of, would defervedly be thought dangerous, and ought to be rejected as fuch: but, with a conftitution of government ' agreeable to the perfection òf human reafon' for a ftandard and criterion, with political maxims the moft eftablifhed, with the foundeft law decifions, and the cleareft informations of *common fenfe* upon, felf-evident propofitions, to juftify any particular meafures concerted for the purpofe of obtaining a recovery from any political malady, and the avoiding of a relapfe; we might then know, that however novel or unexperienced, fuch particular meafures might be, yet that, fo fanctioned, they and the innovations they introduced ought to be adopted :— if, indeed, that could be properly

perly termed an innovation which naturally grew out of the circumftances of the cafe.

12. It is, however, extremely fortunate for us, that making our parliaments *annual,* and our reprefentation *equal,* can neither of them in any fenfe, nor without a direct falfehood, be ftiled innovations. *Both of them were the antient practice of the conftitution.* But parliaments of a longer duration, and that partial reprefentation of the commons we now experience, when firft introduced by kingcraft and court policy, and through the fupinenefs of the commons *were* innovations :— and innovations the more deftructive, as they were not greatly fufpected of danger. That fupinenefs in the commons brought on a relaxation; and relaxation engendered thofe impurities which, at firft, made only a flight and fecret impreffion on the health of the conftitution; then became perceptible and vifibly impaired its ftrength and beauty; but at length, have reduced it to a rotten carcafs. I truft, however, that it is not incurable. The body politic (I mean our own) though, like the natural body it be *fubject* to difeafes and to death, is yet effentially different from it in this refpect;—that, as the natural body grows weaker and weaker from the fucceffive attacks of difeafe, though *ever fo well cured;* and, from its firft formation is perpetually and inevitably tending towards decay; fo on the contrary, the body politic, if but properly cured

F of

of its fucceffive difeafes, is renovated each
time to a degree of vigour more than priftine,
acquiring as it were a continual acceffion of
youth and health, and perpetually adding to
its fources of life. Its natural tendency is
confequently towards all, the immortality
which the duration of this world can afford it.
It is not corporeal. It is not formed from the
duft of the earth. It is purely intellectual;
and its life-fpring is truth. Truth and intellect are eternal. Perhaps the carelefs figura-
tive expreffion of *body* politic, may have con-
tributed very much to the unphilofophical
language commonly ufed, with regard to the
fuppofed certainty that every ftate, like a
human body, muft neceffarily perifh through
infirmities and old age, which *I deny*. I
grant that the beft *may* die of its difeafes; and
that it is not proof againft *fuicide:* but I maintain that it is in its power to live and flourifh
to the end of time: whereas, health itfelf cannot preferve the natural body beyond the
period of nature: it dies of mere time when
no other difeafe ever touches it.

13. We may now proceed to obferve
that the *whole* legiflative body, of king, lords,
and reprefentatives of the commons, is the
full and compleat reprefentative of the *people:*
(§ 7.) and that our conftitution of government, (fuppofing it labouring under no
abufes) is, in its fpirit and principle, a *perfect*
inftitution; being ' agreeable to the perfection

fection of human reafon', and to truth; having
a natural tendency towards perpetuity; and
being rightly calculated to protect the liberty,
property, peace and good name of every
member of the community. By *perfect*, I do
not mean that which it fhall be impoffible to
pervert, that which fools cannot depart from,
nor knaves abufe; and which fhall be neceffarily *exclufive* of evil; but I mean that which
is *not* neceffarily *introductive* of evil. I believe we may venture to call the law of nature
and providence, a *perfect inflitution*; and yet
we fee that it doth not exclude evil; nor *ne-
ceffitate* men to be healthy, wife and virtuous.
On the other hand, *every tyranny* hath been
neceffarily introductive of evil. And in all
free governments which have not had the law
of nature and the perfection of reafon for
their fundamentals, there have been caufes
neceffarily introductive of evil, in proportion
to their refpective defects. And how little
foever chriftianity may be confidered as a
civil inftitution, I cannot but regard it as
abfolutely neceffary towards the conftituting of
a *perfect* political inftitution. It reveals fome
moft important truths in morality, which
the unaided law of nature could never have
made known to us; and it gives man a knowledge of himfelf, and a command over his
paffions, which half-feeing philofophy could
never have taught him. Hence, the fates of
all the free ftates and flourifhing empires

of

of antient and former times, are not to be
looked upon as infallible proofs that our own
ſhall as aſſuredly periſh in procefs of time.
Befides, it hath fared the ſame with all
defective religious, as well as civil eſtabliſh-
ments. The idolatry and polytheifm of the
Aſſyrians, the Medes, Perſians, Greeks and
Romans, all periſhed, as well as their reſpective empires and conſtitutions of government. Does it then follow that the religion
of the Engliſh nation ſhall alſo periſh. We
know it ſhall not periſh. It hath nature and
truth for its foundation : thoſe were built on
error, and with nature had nothing to do.

14. I have dwelt thus long on the nature
and excellence of the Engliſh conſtitution; in
order to ſhew that *it is worth all the regard and
concern we can poſſibly feel for it.* 'Tis the de-
clared opinion of too many, that, ' it is vain to
' attempt a reſtoration of it from its preſent cor-
' rupt, condition and to oppoſe its downfall;'
that ' it is become ripe for abſolute power
' and muſt ſubmit;' that ' the iſland muſt in
' time become a province to ſome new empire;'
that ' this is the inevitable courſe of things,
' and therefore we had better give ourſelves
' no farther trouble, but reſign ourſelves
' patiently to our fate.' I deny every word of
this ſhameful language. It inculcates nothing but vice, folly and meanneſs. Let
Engliſhmen entertain more manly and rational
ſentiments! Thoſe effeminate and daſtardly
notions

notions would of themfelves be fufficient to
bring us into fervitude: for they tell any one
who fhould wifh to become our tyrant, that
we will meet him half way, in order to receive his yoke upon our neck.

15. Having confidered the full reprefentation of the whole people, and the benefits
to be derived from it; let us now contemplate
the reprefentation of the *commons* alone. The
firft and moft natural idea which will occur
to any unprejudiced man, is, that *every individual of them*, whether poffeffed of what
is vulgarly called property, or not, ought to
have a vote in fending to parliament thofe men
who are to act as his reprefentatives; and who
in an efpecial manner, are to be the
guardians of *public freedom*; in which, the
poor, furely, as well as the rich have an
intereft. Although no one of the commons can be originally without a right to
this privilege of a free man; yet, indeed, it
may be juftly forfeited by his offending againft
the laws.

16. Though a man fhould have neither
lands nor gold, nor herds nor flocks; yet he
may have parents and kindred, he may poffefs
a wife and an offspring to be folicitous for.
He hath alfo by birthright a property in the
Englifh conftitution: which, if not unworthy of fuch a bleffing, will be more dear to
him than would be many acres of the foil without it. Thefe are all great ftakes to have at
rifk; and, we muft have odd notions of
                                        juftice,

juſtice, if we do not allow, that they give
him an undoubted right to ſhare in the choice
of thoſe truſtees, into whoſe keeping and protection they are to be committed. Is it not
ſufficient that the poſſeſſions of the plough-
man and mechanick are ſo ſcanty as to afford
them but a ſlender ſecurity againſt penury and
want! Shall we add to the unkindneſs of
fortune, the cruelty of oppreſſion and injuſtice! Conſidering the great utility and
importance of thoſe valuable members of the
ſtate by whoſe manual labours its very ex-
iſtence is preſerved, and its dignity and
grandeur maintained; and on which depend
alſo the affluence, the eaſe, and all the elegan-
cies of the more fortunate claſſes of the people, doubtleſs we ought moſt ſacredly to
ſecure to them whatever they can can call
their own. Their poverty is, ſurely, the
worſt of all reaſons, for ſtripping them of
their natural rights! Let us rather reconcile to
them the many hardſhips of their condition,
by ſhewing them that it doth not degrade
them below the nature of man. If they
have not wherewithal to gratify the pride,
let them at leaſt retain the dignity of human
nature; by knowing they are free, and ſharing
in the privileges inſeparable from liberty. It
is certain that every man who labours with his
hands, has a *property* which is of importance
to the ſtate: for Mr. Locke has admirably
well obſerved that, " every man has a pro-
" perty

" perty in his own perfon ; the labour of his
" body and the work of his hands, we may
" fay are properly his." And farther, let it
be remembered, that the labouring man or
the mechanick can neither have his daily food
nor neceffaries ; nor cloaths to cover him, nor
tools to work with, without paying *taxes* in
abundance; and that it is the fundamental
principle upon which, above all others refpecting property, our liberties depend, that
no man fhall be *taxed* but with his own confent, given either by himfelf or *his reprefentative in parliament* [h]. Hence we find that,
according to *the received doctrine of property*,
no man can be without a right to vote for a reprefentative in the legiflature.

17. But, after all, furely it is not *property*—it cannot be the precarious poffeffion
of clay fields and piles of brick and ftone;
nor of fheep and oxen ; nor of guineas and
fhillings and bank bills ;—nor, indeed, of any
other fpecies of property; which truly con-
ftitutes freedom : no ;—doubtlefs it is the immediate gift of God to all the human fpecies,
by adding *free-will* to *rationality*, in order to
render them beings which fhould be account-
able for their actions. All are by nature free;
all are by nature equal: freedom implies
choice; equality excludes degrees in freedom.

[h] The labourer cannot put a bit of bread into his mouth
without contributing towards the payment of the *land*
tax.

All

All the commons, therefore, have an equal right to vote in the elections of thofe who are to be the guardians of their lives and liberties; and none can be intitled to more than one vote. " In a free ftate," fays Judge Black-ftone in his Commentaries (vol. 1. p. 158) " every man, who is fuppofed a free agent, " ought to be in fome meafure, his own " governor; and therefore a branch at leaft " of the legiflative power fhould refide in the " whole body of the people;" meaning the *commons*. I would not haftily diffent from a re-ceived opinion, efpecially one fupported on great authorities; but yet my own concep-tions of truth oblige me to believe, that *perfonality* is the *fole* foundation of the *right* of being *reprefented:* and that *property* has, in reality, nothing to do in the cafe. The *property* of any one, be it more or be it lefs, is totally involved in the *man*. As belonging to him and to his peace, it is a very fit *object of the attention* of his reprefentative in parlia-ment; but it contributes nothing to his *right* of having that reprefentative. Did the acci-dent of property *conftitute* the right to repre-fentation, 'tis plain, that the property as much as the man, would then be *reprefented*. A member of parliament would, in that cafe, have farms, woods and houfes for his *confti-tuents*, and every other fpecies of property which belonged to his electors. " It may
" be

" be alledged," fays Beccaria, " that the in-
" terefts of commerce fhould be fecured; but
" commerce and property are not the end of
" the focial compact, but the means of ob-
" taining that end:" fo that, by making
property the object of reprefentation, " we
" make," according to him, " the end fub-
" fervient to the means, a parologifm in all
" fcience, and particularly in all politics."

18. When *all* the commons, without diftinction, fhall vote in elections, we fhall then
effectually provide that " not a blade of grafs
" be taxed except with the confent of the
" proprietor:" and we fhall do more; much
more; for guardians will be appointed to
every fpecies of property whatfoever; and to
the poor man's mite, as well as to the rich
ones fuperfluous wealth. Every man's whole
is at a ftake be that more or lefs. Every man
is free; and therefore he ought to vote: no
man, be his property what it may, can be
more than a free man; and therefore no one
is intitled to more than his fingle vote. If a
wealthy perfon is to be indulged with more
votes than one, 'tis evident that, in exact
proportion as this practice fhall prevail, the
value of every poor man's vote will be di-
minifhed. But all fuch ideas are arbitrary
and unjuft, and proceed from our adopting
falfe principles of liberty; as will be ex-
plained hereafter (§ 24). Surely riches give
their poffeffors fo many other advantages, that
G   they

they may be content with their lot, without invading the liberties of the poor!—
not to obferve, that to reftore the right of
voting to the poor, would better fecure the
property of the rich, than any other means
that can be thought of.

The rich man, by the affiftance of *lawyers,*
which his wealth will always procure him,
can defend his property, even while legiflation
is very corrupt: but the poor man, for the
fecurity of his, depends altogether on the
equity and wifdom of legiflation; and therefore, if any difference ought to be made, the
poor man fhould have his reprefentative in the
legiflature, and not the rich one.

19. This, together with an annual parliament, would purify the fountain of legiflation.
And it is better, for even a rich man, to depend upon the purity of legiflation, than upon
the ingenuity of a lawyer.

But farther:—there is yet another argument, in favour of the privilege which the
poor, as well as the rich, ought to have in
voting for members of parliament: and, like
each of the other feparately, furnifhes a full
proof of their right. It is derived from *public
fervices* to the community. He who has lefs
than 40 fhillings *per ann.* in common with him
who hath more, is compellable to contribute
his fhare towards the prefervation of the public peace, the execution of the numerous poor
laws, and the care of our places of public
worfhip,

worſhip, and of the public highways, &c.
ſerving by rotation in the reſpective pariſh
offices of church-warden, overſeer of the
highways, overſeer of the poor, and conſtable.
Is he, I pray, to be only a drudge in the ſervice of the community, and to have no one
privilege which can give him an idea of being
a *free* member of it? When harraſſed by the
duties of an unthankful office into which he
is forced; when fined for ſitting in his own
waggon upon the road; when compelled to
attend the ſummons of a juſtice of the peace
on ſome frivolous miſrepreſentation; is he
not, from his little inſight into the nature of
a national juriſprudence, but too apt to look
upon the law, as a ſnare to the unwary, and an
engine of oppreſſion to the poor; made
by he knows not whom, but, as he takes
for granted certainly deſigned only for the benefit of the rich? Is it not benevolent,
as well as juſt, to allow him that ſhare in
forming the legiſlature, which ſhall give him
more reſpect for the law, and teach him con-
tentment under its reſtraints. Had he annually a vote, for the moſt worthy gentleman he knew in the country to˙ be his
repreſentative, would he not ſee the law and
his own humble ſtation with very different eyes
from what he does now?—The pernicious conſequences of partial and unjuſt laws are
finely repreſented by the Marquis Beccaria in
the perſon of a robber or aſſaſſin, whom he
ſuppoſes to reaſon with himſelf thus: "What

"are

" are thefe laws, that I am bound to refpect,
" which make fo great a difference between
" me and the rich man? He refufes me the
" farthing I afk of him, and excufes himfelf,
" by bidding me have recourfe to labour, with
" which he is unacquainted. Who made
" thefe laws? The rich and the great, who
" never deigned to vifit the miferable hut of
" the poor; who have never yet feen him
" dividing a piece of mouldy bread, amidft
" the cries of his famifhed children and
" the tears of his wife. Let us break thofe
" ties, fatal to the greateft part of mankind,
" and only ufeful to a few indolent tyrants.
" Let us attack injuftice at its fource. I will
" return to my natural ftate of independence.
" I fhall live free and happy on the fruits of
" my courage and induftry. A day of pain
" and repentance may come, but it will be
" fhort; and for an hour of grief I fhall enjoy
" years of pleafure and liberty. King of a
" fmall number as determined as myfelf, I
" will correct the miftakes of fortune; and I
" fhall fee thofe tyrants grow pale and tremble
" at the fight of him, whom, with infulting
" pride, they would not fuffer to rank with
" their dogs and horfes P." Nor, are the
juft pleas of the poor man yet exhaufted.
That which I am going to mention, though
laft, is not the leaft. He takes his conftant

P Effay on crimes and punifhments, p. 110.

chance

chance on a ballot, which is equivalent to taking his regular turn, to ferve his country, as one of its military reprefentatives, in the militia; and an important fervice it is. Here he becomes fubjected to all the reftraints, the labours and feverities of military duty and difcipline; and, in cafe of neceffity, muft be the fhield of his country, and expofe his life in battle for its defence, How comes he to be fubjected to fuch a condition? If it be by laws enacted by men, in whofe election he had no voice, he is a flave. I can conceive no clearer idea of flavery, than for one man to be obliged againft his will to be the foldier of another. Is it *England* or *Pruffia* in which we live. " But, giving up " the point," fays the honeft Burgh [i], in confequence of having adopted a falfe principle, " concerning the right of the poor to vote for members of parliament," &c. This point, however, I can by no means give up. It is the poor man's right : and he who takes it from him is a robber and a tyrant. It is the moft facred of all his rights: and deprived of this, he is degraded below the condition of human nature ; he is no longer a *perfon* but a *thing*. And " liberty is at an end," fays the admirable writer quoted above, " when " ever the laws permit, that, in certain cafes, " a man may ceafe to be a *perfon*, and become

[i] Pol. Difq. vol. I. p. 38.

a *thing*.

" a *thing*. Then will the powerful employ
" their addrefs, to felect from the various
" combinations of civil fociety, all that is in
" their own favour. This is that magic art
" which transforms fubjects into beafts of
" burthen, and which, in the hands of the
" ftrong, is the chain that binds the weak
" and incautious. Thus it is, that in fome
" governments, *where there is all the appear-*
" *ance of liberty"* (mark Englifhmen the
words of this wife Italian!) " tyranny lies
" concealed, and infinuates itfelf into fome
" *neglected corner of the conftitution,* where it
" gathers ftrength infenfibly. Mankind ge-
" nerally oppofe with refolution, the affaults
" of barefaced and open tyranny; but difre-
" gard the *little infect* that gnaws through the
" dike, and opens a fure, though fecret paf-
" fage to inundation." That parliamentary
corruption which, at the revolution, was an
imperceptible embryo, and then a *little infect,*
is at length become a huge, a filthy and
gluttonous monfter. It hath already devoured
the whole dike of our defence, and is now
making its laft unrighteous meal upon its
own vitals : being doomed, if we are tame
enough not to accelerate its fate and ftay the
flood, to perifh by the fame inundation of
defpotifm which it has laboured to let in
upon our liberties.

20. Nothing, then, but an abfolute impracticability, or a care to prevent fome great
public

public incovenience which would overbalance
the advantages propofed from an equal reprefentation, can juftify our departing in any degree, or for the fhorteft period of time, from
thefe principles of freedom and equity, to
the prejudice of any part of the community,
how inconfiderable foever in the eyes of
wealth or pride.

" *Every* Englifhman (fays Sir Tho. Smith)
" is intended to be prefent in parliament,
" either in perfon, or by procuration and
" atturney, of what pre-eminence, ftate,
" dignity, or quality foever he be, from the
" prince to the *loweft* perfon of England. And
" the confent of the parliament is taken to be
" every man's confent."

" The true reafon," fays Judge Blackftone
again (p. 177) " of requiring any qualifica-
" tion, with regard to property, in voters,
" is to exclude fuch perfons as are in fo
" mean a fituation that they are efteemed to
" have no will of their own. If thefe perfons
" had votes, they would be tempted to dif-
" pofe of them under fome undue influence or
" other[i]. This would give a great, an art-
" ful, or a wealthy man, a larger fhare in
" elections than is confiftent with general li-
" berty. If *it were probable* that every man
" would give his vote freely, and without in-

[i] The fame reafoning would be equally conclufive for
thining the houfes of parliament : for a majority of their
members it is evident, grandees, prelates and wealthy
ones as they are, are neverthelefs in fo " *mean* a fituation,"
in fuch poverty of integrity that they are conftantly
" tempted

" fluence of any kind, then, upon the *true*
" *theory* and *genuine principles of liberty*, every
" member of the community, *however poor*,
" fhould have a vote in electing thofe delegates,
" to whofe charge is committed the difpofal of
" his property, his liberty, and his life."

21. If, therefore, it can be fhewn that elections for members of parliament may be fo contrived as to admit of every individual in the community giving his vote; not only with a *probability* of giving it freely, but fo as wholly to prevent the *poffibility* of an undue in-fluence over him; and to fet at defiance all the arts of wealthy and ambitious men; and this moreover without trouble, difficulty or ex-pence; it is to be hoped, if juftice be not banifhed from amongft us, that the practice of the conftitution fhall no longer be kept at variance with the theory, but that millions ᵏ of men now difqualified by our unconfti-tutional ftatutes, fhall be reinftated in this their undoubted, as their unalienable right. And it might alfo be hoped, that it might not be an infuperable objection to fuch a mode of electing, fhould it render bribery and corruption totally impracticable; and put a certain end to all tumultuary proceedings, and to thofe filthy and fcandalous immoralities

" tempted to difpofe of their votes under fome undue in-
" fluence or other;" and we accordingly find that this gives " artful men a larger fhare" in parliamentary di-vifions " than is confiftent with general liberty."

ᵏ I beg pardon: *only* one million four hundred and eighty thoufand,

which,

which, at our prefent elections, are fo deftructive to the morals of the people.

22. Borough qualifications to vote, differ-
ing fo widely one from another, I fhall here
make no farther remark upon them, than to
remind my reader that they are all *arbitrary*;
and do none of them make any juft diftinction
between free-men and thofe, who for any
juft caufe, have forfeited their freedom.

23. In your counties, the diftinction is
equally arbitrary and *more unjuft* than in moft
boroughs, as it disfranchifes a greater proportion of free men. Might not that power
which drew this arbitrary line at *forty fhillings*,
have drawn it, or may it not hereafter draw it,
at any other limit whatfoever ? How often
are we put in mind, by the numerous friends
of undue influence, that forty *fhillings* in the
reign of Henry the fixth, were equal to as
many *pounds* of our prefent money ? And what
is the inference we are taught to draw from
this obfervation? We certainly may, on fuch
principles, live to fee, not only our line of
freedom drawn thus arbitrarily - at fuch a
point, as to exclude nine in ten, or nineteen
in twenty, of the prefent fmall number of
voters; but to have, to the idea of a qualification from *wealth*, the doctrine of *proportion* alfo introduced; whereby we fhould
be compleatly in the power of a few citizens
of overgrown fortunes; and confequently
our happy fyftem of government overthrown.
We have juft beheld an important revolution
H   in

in the government of our Eaft India Company
effected by the joint operation of thefe very
means. It hath at the fame time afforded a
notable inftance of fome mens principles; and
how little fcrupulous they are as to the means
of accomplifhing their defigns. In that company, the line of freedom had been drawn
ever fince its eftablifhment, at a monied qualification of five hundred pounds. But this
rule no longer anfwering the purpofes of thofe
who aimed to make the affairs of the company
fubfervient to their defpotic views, they firft,
by corruption, intimidation and undue influence, contract the limits of freedom, fo as
to include for the future only thofe who
fhould hold one thoufand pounds in ftock;
and then, to complete the bufinefs, they
give the wealthieft ftockholders an additional
number of votes, in *proportion* to their greater
property. I have heard this doctrine of proportion actually propofed, as an improvement
in parliamentary elections : and that it fhould
be adopted doubtlefs is the ardent wifh of
thofe who took fo much pains to eftablifh it
in the cafe before us. Let us fuppofe, for
the fake of argument, that it *was* adopted; as
well as their other favourite point of raifing
the qualification to forty pounds *per ann.*
and that every additional forty pounds *per ann.*
fhould give an additional vote. Such a law
would at once fweep away nine in ten at
leaft of your prefent fmall number of voters;
and, at the fame time, it would annex to an
eftate

eftate of 400l. *per ann.* 10 votes; to one of 4000l. *per ann.* it would give 100 votes; and a landed property of 40,000l. *per ann.* (which is far fhort of what commoners have poffeffed) would then give its poffeffor no lefs than 1000 votes. Thus we fee the errors into which we might be drawn, by admitting *property,* to confer the right of being reprefented; and *wealth,* that of being reprefented in a tenfold or a thoufand-fold proportion. A right of being reprefented, every man owes to God, who gave him his freedom; but many a man owes his wealth to the devil. It ought, in that cafe, to give him a rope, rather than a reprefentative.

24. Although I would warn my country-men at large by the fate of the proprietors of Eaft India ftock; and think I am well war-ranted in believing that the movers in that bufinefs would gladly play a fimilar game in the nation; I do not mean to draw an *un-limited* comparifon between the government of a little feparate trading community, and of the great civil community of the public. The *freedoms* of their refpective members depend on principles effentially different. An in-creafe of *wealth,* not the prefervation of *civil liberty,* is the grand object in a trading com-pany. So *property* and not *perfonality* (con-trary to the rule in *civil fociety*) is here the *fole* foundation of a right in the individual to be reprefented, and freedom may be *conftituted*

by

by any *arbitrary criterion* which the parties concerned fhall agree upon. In *civil liberty* which is a *natural* blefling: as heretofore obferved, (§. 1. 3.) there muft be *equality*. This is not the cafe with regard to the *freedom* of the *trading company*, which is altogether *artificial* and depends folely upon *property*; which may be, and always has been, very *un*equally diftributed. Hence, in a *trading* fociety, reprefentation may juftly be *proportioned* to property[1]. And had the Eaft India Company, by a fair majority without undue influence of any kind, new modelled their government, and changed their line of freedom, there could not have been, on the fcore of juftice, any objection to their proceeding; how much foever it might have been liable to exception in point of prudence. It will, however, fcarcely be thought reafonable, or, conducing to the good of the *public* in that company, that a proprietor poflefling nine hundred and ninety-nine pounds fhould be judged unworthy of having a voice in appointing guardians to fo much property; who are, at the fame time, to be *factors* for ad-

[1] Had the truly patriotic author of the Political Difquifitions adverted to thefe neceffary diftinctions, he would not have thought the regulation in the Eaft India Company of having votes in proportion to wealth, " worthy of imitation;" (p. 49 vol. I.) except *by other trading companies only*.

venturing

venturing it in trade to the extreme parts of
Aſia.

25. The foregoing diſtinctions between
the principles of government in *trading* and
in *civil* communities ſhould be carefully attended to; in order that we may never be
miſled by artful reaſonings from the *former*,
applied to the *latter*. That which may be an
excellent regulation or ſyſtem for the *increaſe*
of *wealth*, may by no means be proper for the
ſecurity of *freedom*. And the laws of a ſmall
trading community aſſociated for that particular purpoſe, making all the while a diminutive
part, and being ſubject to the laws of a great
civil community, are not very likely to be of
ſo liberal and comprehenſive a nature as to be
well calculated for national purpoſes.

Mr. Burgh concludes his chapter, on,
' What would be adequate parliamentary re-
preſentation,' thus; " The moſt adequate
" plan for forming an aſſembly of repreſen-
" tatives, would be, for every county, in-
" cluding the cities, boroughs, cinque ports,
" or univerſities it happens to contain, to ſend
" in a proportion of the 513 anſwering to its
" *contribution to the public expence.*" But a
little conſideration will ſhew us that we cannot poſſibly come at this proportion. The
landholders and other original poſſeſſors of
taxable property, only advance the reſpective
taxes; they are really *paid* by the conſumers
only. The land-tax of Leiceſterſhire, Lincoln-
ſhire

shire and Nottinghamshire, is paid by the thousands of manufacturers in Derbyshire, Lancashire and Yorkshire, who eat the beef and mutton, and consume the malt of those counties. And so it is with all other commodities. After the taxes upon them are *advanced* by the original possessors, a commercial circulation through a thousand various channels distributes them to all parts of the kingdom; where the taxes are finally and *solely* paid by the *consumers*; and it is clear that, where there are the greatest numbers of consumers, there must be *the greatest contribution in taxes, to the public expence*. But Sir Isaac Newton himself could not calculate these proportions, from tax books, with a thousandth part of the accuracy that our church wardens can give it us, from their parish rolls of the inhabitants. Thus we see, that an arbitrary and unjust rule of proceeding would bear no degree of comparison, in point of simplicity and facility, with the only rule which is founded on equity and the true principles of our free constitution.

26. Whenever the *first principle* of any reasoning is false we are navigating without a compass, and can have no criterion of rectitude as we go along, but must for ever be liable to error and abuse. Had we never departed from the true principle, of considering *every* member of the community as a free-man, we had done right. But when we would once form

an *arbitrary* definition of freedom, who fhall
fay what it ought to be; Ought freedom rather to be annexed to forty pence, or forty
fhillings, or forty pounds *per annum?* Or
why not to four hundred, or four thoufand?
But, indeed, fo long as money is to be the
meafure of it, 'twill be *impoffible* to know who
ought, and who ought not, to be free. According to my apprehenfion, we might as
well make the poffeffion of forty fhillings
per annum, the proof of a man's being *rational*,
as of his being *free*. There is juft as much
fenfe in one as in the other.

27. Provided the foregoing reflections be
admitted to be juft, it muft neceffarily follow,
that the commons of this kingdom have
at the prefent time, nothing better than a
mock reprefentation of fo dangerous a nature,
that nothing fhort of the conftant miraculous
interpofition of heaven in their favour, can
poffibly fave them from a fpeedy fubjection to
arbitrary power; except they will rouze themfelves from their lethargy, and form to themfelves fuch a reprefentation as, by the eternal
principles of freedom in general, and the exprefs doctrine of their own conftitution in particular, they are entitled to. It is to be hoped
that their tables of indulgence and beds of
down, and the captivating charms of pleafure,
have not fo melted down the once glorious
fpirit of the Britifh nation, and funk it to
fuch a degree in floth and effeminacy, that all
its

its powers of felf-exertion are paft and gone
for ever! Surely, what I have taken to be only
the lethargy of eafe and idlenefs, is not in
reality that ftupifying coma, which is the fure
prefage of approaching death!

28. Is it not notorious that feats in the
houfe of commons are confidered as a. property and an inheritance? Do they not pafs
from hand to hand, as appendages to eftates in
old houfes? And are they not bought and fold
like ftock in Change Alley? Is there no placed or
penfioned *peer*, who hath fix, feven or eight
members to reprefent him, and him only, in
the houfe of *commons*; while *one million four
hundred and eighty thoufand* of the commons
themfelves are not thought worthy of a fingle
vote amongft them? (See Sect. 32.) We know
there are fuch peers. Nay, do we not know
alfo that feats in parliament have been paid
away as gaming-debts, from fleeced and needy
lords to tavern waiters and common gamblers[m]?
Blufh Englifhmen, blufh, if there be a fpark
of manhood left in your compofition! And,
when ridiculed with the title of free men

[m] Of a Chefhire gentleman there is this anecdote.
His Borough gives him fome offence concerning a propofed election. He fends them his black footman, with
a peremptory order to elect him their reprefentative. The
corporation draw up a petition; in which they humbly
afk his honour's pardon, and affure him that, if he will in-
dulge them with a *white* man, they fhall not regard whom
or what he may be, but will return him and be thankful.

hide

hide your ignominious heads!—But perhaps all
thefe things are right :—perhaps it is alfo right
for the two or three cottagers of Bramber and
Dunwich, and the lord of the borough of Old
Sarum, where there is neither houfe nor inhabitant, to fend to parliament as many members as your moft opulent cities; while many
towns of the firft manufacturing confequence
have not a reprefentative! Perhaps it would,
moreover, be right to lay afide the whole farce
of elections, and for the minifter to call up fuch
faithful commons as he knew would fooneft
difpatch his bufinefs!—Perhaps, I fay all
this, and more might be right! Perhaps it
might not be thought too much, were we,
like the good fubjects of Denmark, humbly
to intreat the king to take the fole trouble of
managing our affairs, and to make ufe of our
lives and fortunes at his difcretion and good
pleafure!——Could Englifhmen in general be
brought to think fo; and fhould there be no
poffibility of convincing them of their error;
it furely would be no crime, after fhedding a
few tears of natural affection ill placed, to re-
nounce an undeferving country for ever; and
to feek for liberty amongft any other people
who had fenfe enough to know its value, and
courage to defend it at every hazard. May
we not, with great reafon, conclude that
the time is not far off, in which the character
of the nation fhall be decidedly fixed; either
by manifefting that its antient fterling fpirit

I   hath

hath *not* forfaken it; or elfe, by difcovering that it hath indeed, as there is too much reafon to apprehend, imported at once the pufillanimity, together with the fpoils of India; and the cringing fervility, together with the frivolous fopperies and loofe principles, of Italy and France? Should even its virtues and its wifdom be no more; one might think that even felf-love alone and a defire of eafe, might teach it to prefer affluence to indigence, liberty to flavery. But if there be no principle in nature, active enough to put us in motion for our own good;—if nothing but an opera or a mafquerade, a horfe-race or a pack of cards, be worth our attention;—if we be fo venal and abandoned, as to prefer proftitution and loofe pleafures, to independency and the public weal; we have not manly fenfibility enough left to feel any indignity: but fhall continue to fuffer a neft of court fycophants and public plunderers, impudently to call themfelves our reprefentatives; and to exercife fuch powers, as will foon enable their employers to throw off the mafk, and contemptuoufly to forbid us even to utter that poor confolatory word, *reprefentation,* with the mere found of which we have fo long contented ourfelves. It would, at the approach of fuch a period, be time, for every one who had not fortitude enough to follow liberty acrofs the Atlantic, to forget all that belongs to the great character of a

free

free man, and to learn the bafe and fawning arts of a willing flave; for fuch a difpofition and fuch fentiments would then beft fuit with his fallen condition. A race fo utterly degenerate as to caft away liberty and put on chains at the bidding of their own fervants, would merit no better treatment than to be fpurned and trampled on by the beaftly foot of defpotifm.

29. Suffering as we do, from a deep parliamentary corruption, it is no time to tamper with filly correctives, and trifle away the life of public freedom; but we muft go to the bottom of the wound and cleanfe it thoroughly; we muft once more infufe into the conftitution, the vivyfying fpirit of liberty, and expel the very laft dregs of this poifon. Annual parliaments and an equal reprefentation of the commons are the only fpecifics in this cafe: and they would effect a radical cure. That a houfe of commons, formed as ours is, fhould maintain feptennial elections, and laugh at every other idea, is no wonder. The wonder is, that the Britifh nation, which, but the other day, was the greateft nation on earth, fhould be fo eafily laughed out of its liberties.

30. As to the hope of removing the evils of a feptennial, by changing it for a triennial, parliament, I confefs it appears to me altogether illufive. On a fuperficial view, fuch a meafure promifes fome beneficial confequences; and it is not uncommon to fup-

pofe,

pofe, that it would at leaft leffen our parliamentary evils in the fame proportion as
there is between the refpective numbers of
years of their durations. But now, that corruption is reduced to a fcience, and this
fcience is fo thoroughly underftood by minifters, I fhould fear that, if it made any difference at all, it muft be for the worfe.
The whole queftion may be reduced to
this;—would it be poffible to corrupt
a triennial parliament? If it *would* be
poffible, — as, indeed, who doubts but it
would, then the evil would in fact be aug-
mented, inftead of being abated; becaufe the
additional difficulty and trouble, would neceffarily caufe an increafe of expence. Corruption muft be made abfolutely impracticable, by means of annual elections and an
equal reprefentation. There feems to be, in
my poor opinion, no fenfe nor fafety in any
other meafure.

31. That man, amongft the oppofition
to the prefent ruinous men and meafures of
the court, who fhall not immediately pledge
himfelf to the public, by the moft explicit
declarations and the moft facred affurances, to
exert himfelf to the utmoft of his power and
abilities, and perpetually, fo long as he fhall
live, in attempting to bring about a thorough
and compleat parliamentary reformation; and
fhall not inftantly fet about it, in preference
to every other confideration; is, in my humble

ble opinion, nothing better than a factious demagogue; who cares not that his country be funk in the pit of perdition, fo long as he can but hope to come in for a fhare of power and plunder. On the other hand; fuch declarations, affurances and actions, would make him appear, in the eyes of the nation, as a guardian angel: and they would be ready to kifs the very ground on which he trod, in reverence of his virtue and patriotifm. A handful of fuch honeft men, acting in concert, might fave their country; in fpight of a tyrannical adminiftration, and a venal parliament. But if the members of oppofition have fuch *feparate* views and defigns, when only *one* view and *one* plan ought to actuate them, that they will not form this union, and act in concert for the falvation of their country, let them not tell us, any longer, of their love of liberty and of their public fpirit. The lofs of America, followed by an unequal war, together with all the fatal confequences they threaten, great and dreadful as fuch evils may juftly be confidered, are as a mere nothing, a very duft in the balance, compared with the total lofs of our liberties, which muft enfue, and foon too, unlefs a parliamentary reformation take place: and I will add, that immediate reformation, in that particular, might,—it would—but nothing elfe can, re-unite us with our American colonies; as their kindred, their allies, and monopolizers of

their

their commerce; on terms more mutually
and permanently beneficial, than could have
subfifted while we ftood in the relation to
each other of fovereign and dependent ftates.
But, to amufe us with any other meafures,
than thofe of a thorough parliamentary reformation, for alleviating our national mis-
fortunes, would be nothing better than to
prune away fome of the leaves and luxuriant
fhoots of corruption, inftead of hewing down
the accurfed trunk, and tearing up the roots.
It muft be exterminated root and branch, or
we perifh.

32. Thofe who now claim the *exclufive*
right, of fending to parliament the 513 reprefentatives for about fix millions, confift of
lefs than twenty thoufand perfons[n]; and 254
of thefe reprefentatives are elected by 5723[o].
Nothing but a delegation of this truft from
the faid fix millions, or at leaft a majority of
them, could poffibly have given them this
right. They never were fo delegated. Had
even the anceftors of thefe lefs than twenty
thoufand citizens, been fo delegated, by the
anceftors of the fix millions, yet even that
could not, in the leaft, have bettered their
title. 'Their pretended rights are, many of

[n] This number was taken through inadvertency.
There is fome difficulty in afcertaining the true number;
but the reader is requefted to make it 200,000. The
main conclufions will ftill remain in full force.
[o] Polit. Difq. chap. 4.

them,

them, derived from *royal favour*; some, from
antient usage and prescription; and some
indeed from act of parliament: but neither
the most authentic acts of royalty, nor precedent, nor prescription, nor even parliament,
can establish any flagrant injustice;—much less
can they strip one million four hundred and
eighty thousand people of an unalienable
right, to vest it in one seventy.fifth part of
their number [p]. The true, and indeed the
only, operation of these several authorities
hath been, in the case before us, not to *confer*,
but to *take away* a right. The selected persons had originally this right in the most
ample and absolute degree inherent in them-
selves, in common with their fellow citizens:
so that no exercise of legislative power nor of
regal authority [q] could possibly *confer* it, or

[p] 4)6,000,000 souls
   1,500,000 males competent
     20,000 Voters at present
  1,480,000 Competent men who are deprived of the
              right of voting.
20,000)1,500,000
      75
And it is probable that the 1,480,000 *consumers* contribute towards the public expence in about the same proportion as they bear in numbers to the 20,000 : that is
about three guineas and a half to a shilling.—

[q] ' Kings may make lords, and corporations, which
' corporations may send their burgesses to parliament,'
says N: Bacon. The annotator observes, on this,
' Though the king can make corporations, yet he can-
' not give them a right to be represented in parliament
' without the commons consent! Pol. Dif. vol. I. p. 66.

even

even improve it. They have however *de-prived* the reft of the community of this their inherent right.

33. The very idea of the right we are treating of, originating from, or being dependent upon, the *pleafure of the crown*, is glaringly abfurd. In the times, however, during which fo illegal an ufe was made of the prerogative [r], the inconveniences were not felt as they are by us, nor were thofe frightful confequences which now threaten with a fpeedy diffolution the whole frame of our conftitution, much forefeen by the commons; or we may prefume they would have been guarded againft. But, indeed, we muft allow that there were but very few periods within thofe times, in which the commons were in any condition to have held fuch a conteft with the crown; or when the moft dutiful petitions or remonftrances, on fuch a fubject, would have obtained them any re-drefs. More wife and more virtuous than other men muft be that prince (a very rare cafe indeed!) who will yield up one particle of power, however unjuft, except from neceffity

---

[r] We now a days think it a tolerable ftretch of the prerogative when a king pours into the houfe of *peers* a dozen members at a time: but if the title of our boroughs to fend their two members each to parliament be *a good one*, then his prefent majefty may add to the houfe of *commons* as many members as he pleafes. James the Ift. privileged 14 boroughs, which fent into the houfe 27 members.

or

or compulsion.—Although we have reason to believe that the commons were not sufficiently foresighted, yet we may safely conclude that our princes knew in general what they were doing, when they called upon so many of the petty boroughs within *their own hereditary private domain,* to send up members to the great council of the nation. But they not only called up whom they pleased; for they discontinued, as occasion served, the calling up of others: thus " removing, at their " pleasure, the landmarks of the constitution, " and wounding it in its most vital part '." The two and twenty towns which had their representatives in the parliament of Edward I. but which were afterwards deprived, by *the mere will of the crown,* did not many of them, we may safely take for granted, lie within the *Duchy of Cornwall.*

34. How parliamentary representation became so inadequate as it is, we may see in the 5th chap. of Political Disquisitions : but the author does not shew us how our kings came by the *right* of calling up to parliament *only* whom they pleased; sometimes allowing towns, and even counties, a representation in parliament, and sometimes not, as suited with their own purposes. Nor has he, nor any other author, shewn us by what virtue a *royal* charter can authorize half a dozen of

' Mr. Wilkes's speech in the House of Commons, 2J March, 1776.

K   the

the *commons,* exclufive to elect legiflators for many hundred times their own number[s]. How far foever fuch charters may confer *other* exclufive privileges, let lawyers determine; but that they can give any exclufive right to the people in our boroughs, of exclufively voting for members of parliament, *I pofitively deny.* The very idea, I muft repeat, is abfurd. The king has no right, by his prerogative, to fummon *any* parliament which fhall not be with regard to the lower houfe, an actual reprefentation[t] of *all* the commons: fo, it is evident that the cuftomary writs, directed to about twenty thoufand electors, who compofe only a 75th part of the commons, notwithftanding their antiquity, are unconftitutional and unobligatory; being vitiated *ab initio* by

---

[s] A corporation of 15 members, as Bramber for inftance, elects as many members of parliament as fall to the proportion of 5848 perfons, who make 390 times their number. And Bramber is not the fmalleft of our boroughs.

[t] Since a *virtual* reprefentation in the houfe of commons was fo learnedly argued to extend to three millions of people beyond the Atlantic; we may expect that it will be moft unmercifully crammed down the throats of poor Englifhmen, (provided they do not fpit it out,) as being every whit as good, as wholefome and nourifhing, as a real reprefentation. But, to thofe authors who fhall endeavour to palm it upon us, we may fay to the fame purpofe as the managers in Hogarth write to the prodigal author, who, in hopes of relieving his own beggary and fupplying his extravagancies, had troubled them with a dramatic piece, made up of the crude conceptions of a vicious brain : 'We have tried your farce, and find it will not do.'

their

their total want of reafon and equity. 'Tis a
precedent to be quoted only to be over-ruled.
It was originally an ufurpation on an inherent
and unalienable right, and no prefcription
can make it law. " It is," fays an excellent
writer, " a fundamental principle in our con-
" ftitution, and was, until the reign of Henry
" VI. the invariable practice of it, that the
" property of the people, *not one man excepted,*
" could not be granted but by his own con-
" fent, given by himfelf or his reprefentative
" chofen by himfelf. It was upon this princi-
" ple that, until that reign, every man in the
" kingdom gave his vote, or had a right to give
" his vote, for the election of reprefentative,
" on whom that power was devolved. The
" 7th of Henry IV. made upon complaint of
" this right having been difturbed, ordains,
" that *all the people* fhall elect indifferently.
" Their being refidents in the county is the
" only qualification required. It was not
" until the 8th year of Henry VI. that the
" poffeffion of forty fhillings *per annum,* &c[u].

35. Judge Blackftone informs us that
" parliament is coeval with the kingdom
" itfelf [v]:" that " we have inftances of its
" meeting in the reigns of Ina, Offa and
" Ethelbert[w]:" that " upon the true theory

---

[u] Appeal to the juftice and interefts of the people of
Great Britain, in the prefent difputes with America, p. 5.
[v] Vol. I. p. 149.
[w] Ibid, 148.

" and

" and genuine principles of liberty every
" member of the community, however poor,
" fhould have a vote ˣ;" and that " every
" man, who is fuppofed a free-agent, ought
" to be, in fome meafure, his own governor;
" and therefore a branch at leaft of the
" legiflative power fhould refide in the whole
" body of the people," meaning commons ʸ.

36. Where then is the foundation for that
monopoly of reprefentation now enjoyed by
the voters of our defpicable boroughs, and of
forty fhilling freeholders, to the injury and
difgrace of the nation at large ?—It hath no
foundation. It ought inftantly to be abolifhed.
Every day it is fuffered to continue, the nation
is facrificed to a handful of venal wretches,
who conftantly fell its liberties, at every
election, for the term of the enfuing parliament. The deprived perfons, who in fact
make the body of the nation, are in duty
bound to do themfelves and their pofterity
right, by refuming this ineftimable franchife
into their own hands.

37. But, we are told of *difficulties* in
making our reprefentation equal; and of *inconveniences* in parliaments wherein there
fhould be no court influence. Since we have
got over the difficulties of electing our thirty
two thoufand *military* reprefentatives, the mi-

ˣ Vol. I. p. 171.
ʸ Ibid. 158.

litia;

litia; and that, by balloting a due proportion of ferviceable men throughout the kingdom ᶻ; we need not, I think, defpair of being *able* to choofe five hundred and thirteen *civil* repre-fentatives, whenever we may have the *will* to fet about it. As to the other objection to our plan of reforming, I own it puzzles me. It comes from Mr. Hume, who is fo re-fpectable as an hiftorian, a philofopher and moralift; and, therefore, it is a ferious one:

ᶻ The plan for defending this country by a militia, was called by the late Earl of Chefterfield " a filly fcheme which muft be dropped." See his letter to his fon, Sept. 23, 1757. We have neverthelefs experienced it to be a wife fcheme, and feen it brought to great perfection; in oppofition to very bitter and indefatigable parliamentary enemies, and even to minifters. In addition to a proftitute parliament, they want nothing more than a ftanding army, in order to fubvert the laft remains of liberty. And his lordfhip expreffes himfelf no lefs contemptuoufly of annual parliaments. In letter 106 vol. 2. he fays—" The " houfe of commons is ftill very unanimous : there was " a little *popular fquib* let off this week, in a motion of " Sir John Glyn's, feconded by Sir John Philips, for " annual parliaments. It was *a very cold fcent*, and put " an end to by a divifion of 190 to 70." But we muft not be furprifed at fuch fentiments from a man who could write to his fon as follows : " Yefterday morning Mr. ** " came to me, from lord Halifax, to afk me whether I " thought you would approve of vacating your feat in par- " liament, during the remainder of it, upon a valuable " confideration, meaning *money*. My anfwer was, that I " really did not know your difpofition upon that fubject; " but that I knew you would be very willing, in general, " to accommodate them, as far as lay in your power. " That your election, to my knowledge, had coft you " two thoufand pounds; that this parliament had not fat
" above

fo ferious, indeed, that I am at a lofs for any other anfwer to it, but—to burft out a laughing in Mr. Hume's face. It would do no great harm, however, methinks, *juft to try the experiment.* The inconvenience of too rigid a virtue, might poffibly be remedied in this indulgent age, if it fhould be experienced. Mr. Hume will, I dare fay, allow me a little fcepticifm as to the juftnefs and weight of his objection; which I muft tell him, in plain terms, I never can believe until I fhall know *by experience* [a].

. What is a houfe of commons, if it be not a check upon the crown, in which refide all the executive powers of government? Thefe executive powers would be more fatal to fociety than plague, peftilence and famine, except a fufficient check upon them fhould be provided. This is a truth we find written

" above half its time ; and that, for my part, I approved
" of the meafure well enough" (well done old bawd !)
" provided you had an equivalent," &c. vol. 2. *Lett.* 161.
" In one of our converfations here, this time twelve-
" month, I defired him to fecure you a feat in the new
" parliament, &c. fince that, I have heard no more of
" it; which made me look out for fome venal borough :
" and I fpoke to a borough jobber, and offered five-and-
" twenty hundred pounds for a fecure feat in parliament ;
" but he laughed at my offer, and faid, that there was no
" fuch thing as a borough to be had now; for that the
" rich Eaft and Weft-Indians had fecured them all, at the
" rate of three thoufand pounds at leaft; but many at
" four thoufand ; and two or three, that he knew, at five
" thoufand." *Vol.* 2d. *Lett.* 193.
   [a] Mr. Hume was living when this was written.

in

in the tears and the blood of mankind in
every age and country. Is this check, then,
to be appointed by him whom it is to curb?
Or, when appointed by others, is he, by
court influence, to convert this curb into
an impetus of that very power it was intended to counterbalance and reftrain?—
Nonfenfe!—And to put up with fuch a mock
reprefentation as cannot be proof againft court
influence, is juft as rational as to tether a bull
with a *hay*-band.

38. The objections to an equality of reprefentation have not been wholly confined to
minifterial writers, nor, indeed, have any of
them urged them with fo much ability as
a very popular writer. I mean Junius.

" I am convinced," fays he, " that, if
" fhortening the duration of parliaments
" (which in effect is keeping the reprefenta-
" tive under the rod of the conftituent) be not
" made the bafis of our new parliamentary
" jurifprudence, other checks or improve-
" ments fignify nothing. On the contrary,
" if this be made the foundation, other mea-
" fures may come in aid, and, as auxiliaries,
" be of confiderable advantage. Lord Cha-
" tham's project, for inftance, of increafing
" the number of knights of fhires, appears
" to me admirable.—As to cutting away the
" rotten boroughs, I am as much offended
" as any man at feeing fo many of them un-
" der the direct influence of the crown, or at
" the

" the difpofal of private perfons. Yet, I own,
" I have both doubts and apprehenfions, in
" regard to the remedy you propofe. I fhal
" be charged perhaps with an unufual want of
" political intrepidity, when I honeftly con-
" fefs to you, that I am ftartled at the idea of
" fo extenfive an amputation.—In the firft
" place, I queftion the power, *de jure,* of the
" legiflature to disfranchife a number of bo-
" roughs, upon the general ground of im-
" proving the conftitution. There cannot
" be a doctrine more fatal to the liberty and
" property we are contending for, than that,
" which confounds the idea of a fupreme and
" an arbitrary legiflature; I need not point out
" to you the fatal purpofes, to which it has
" been, and may be applied. If we are fin-
" cere in the political creed we profefs, there
" are many things, which we ought to affirm,
" cannot be done by king, lords and commons.
" Among thefe I reckon the disfranchifing of
" boroughs with a general view of improve-
" ment. I confider it as equivalent to rob-
" bing the parties concerned of their freehold,
" of their birth-right. I fay that, although
" this birth-right may be forfeited, or the
" exercife of it fufpended in particular cafes,
" it cannot be taken away by a general law,
" for any real or pretended purpofe of im-
" proving the conftitution. Suppofing the
" attempt made, I am perfuaded you cannot
" mean that either King, or Lords fhould
                                    " take

" take an active part in it. A bill which only
" touches the reprefentation of the people,
" muft originate in the houfe of commons.
" In the formation and mode of paffing it,
" the exclufive right of the commons muft be
" afferted as fcrupuloufly, as in the cafe of
" a money-bill. Now fir, I fhould be glad
" to know by what kind of reafoning it can
" be proved, that there is a power vefted in
" the reprefentative to deftroy his immediate
" conftituent: from whence could he poffibly
" derive it ? A courtier, I know, will be
" ready to maintain the affirmative. The
" doctrine fuits him exactly, becaufe it gives
" an unlimited operation to the influence of
" the crown. But we, Mr. Wilkes, ought
" to hold a different language. It is no an-
" fwer to me to fay, that the bill, when it
" paffes the houfe of commons, is the act of
" the majority, and not the reprefentatives of
" the particular boroughs concerned. If the
" majority can disfranchife ten boroughs,
" why not twenty, why not the whole king-
" dom ? Why fhould not they make their
" own feats in parliament for life?—When the
" feptennial act paffed, the legiflature did
" what, apparently and palpably, they had
" no power to do; but they did more than
" people in general were aware of: they, in
" effect, disfranchifed the whole kingdom
" for four years.

L

" For argument's fake, I will now fuppofe
" that the expediency of the meafure, and
" the power of parliament are unqueftionable.
" Still you will find an infurmountable diffi-
" culty in the execution. When all your in-
" ftruments of amputation are prepared, when
" the unhappy patient lies bound at your
" feet, without the poffibility of refiftance,
" by what infallible rule will you direct the
" operation ? — When you propofe to cut
" away the rotten parts, who can tell us
" what parts are perfectly found ?—Are there
" any certain limits, in fact or theory, to in-
" form you at what point you muft ftop, at
" what point the mortification ends? To a
" man fo capable of obfervation and reflection
" as you are, it is unneceffary to fay all that
" might be faid upon the fubject. Befides
" that I approved highly of Lord Chatham's
" idea of infufing a portion of new health into
" the conftitution to enable it to bear its in-
" firmities; (a brilliant expreffion, and full
" of intrinfick wifdom) other reafons concur
" in perfuading me to adopt it. [b]"

39. In quoting the foregoing paffage himfelf, he adds, with a genuine magnanimity;
" The man who fairly and compleatly an-
" fwers this argument, fhall have my thanks
" and applaufe. My heart is already with
" him.—I am ready to be converted.—I ad-

[b] Letter to Mr. Wilkes.

mire

" mire his morality, and would gladly fub-
" fcribe to the articles of his faith.—Grate-
" full, as I am, to the Good Being, whofe
" bounty has imparted to me this reafoning
" intellect, whatever it is, I hold myfelf pro-
" portionably indebted to him, from whofe
" inlightened underftanding another ray of
" knowledge communicates to mine. But
" neither fhould I think the moft exalted
" faculties of the human mind, a gift worthy
" of the divinity; nor any affiftance, in the
" improvement of them, a fubject of gratitude
" to my fellow creature, if I were not fatis-
" fied, that really to inform the underftand-
" ing corrects and enlarges the heart ᶜ."

40. I hope the reader thinks that his argument is already anfwered : but I will make
fome remarks upon his particular words.

Firft, then, in anfwer to his query, concerning which are the rotten parts of the unhappy patient propofed to be amputated; I
would, with much deference, take leave to
remark, that this allufion, which is fuggefted
from the practice of bribing, commonly
called *corrupting*, does not furnifh us (as is
too common with the language of allufion)
with a correct idea of the nature of the cafe.
But I make no fcruple to affert, that *juft fo
much* of our mode of electing, as operates
to the exclufion of any individual man from

ᶜ Letter to Mr. Wilkes.

L 2   giving

giving his vote, is defective and unfair; and therefore ought to be altered. The numbers who now elect, with respect to those who are excluded, (admitting the first to be 20,000, and the whole number intitled, to be 1,500,000) are in the proportion of 1 to 75 : so that we say, with some precision, that the rottenness extends to 74 parts in 75. Dividing 1,500,000 by 513, the number of the members, we find that every member ought to be the representative of 2924 persons, and ought at least to have the votes of a majority of that number, or 1463, in order to intitle him to a seat in the house of commons. Can Junius, then, call it the birthright of the lord of the borough of Old Sarum, to be the exclusive elector of two members of parliament, who ought to represent 5848 of the commons ? or of the nine electors of Grampound to send as many members as make the due proportion for 650 times their number? If no free man be disfranchised by admitting *every* man to vote, I hope we cannot, with propriety, say that any borough is *disfranchised.* I mean not to *abridge,* but to *extend,* the limits of freedom. I have already proved (§ 32, 33, 34.) that no individuals, nor bodies corporate, can possibly have any right to elect a parliament to the exclusion of their fellow citizens. If the right of voting be restored to all the rest, and *still retained* by the *lord* of *Old Sarum,* by the voters of

Gram-

Grampound, and every other petty borough, how can they be robbed " of their freehold," of " their birth-right." The birth-right of a *borough* is a phrafe I cannot underftand; but it is becaufe I hold facred the birth-rights of *men,* that I would have *every* man vote; and deny, that a *few* can have a birth-right to appoint legiflators for the *many.* Were indeed our general monopolizing fyftem to be continued; and yet, fome boroughs lopped off, as rotten branches, while others continued on their prefent foot, I grant this would be an arbitrary proceeding, as being without any fixed rule of juftice: but I talk not of *boroughs—*I talk of *men.*

41. I think him perfectly right with regard to that tenacioufnefs touching any bill for new modelling reprefentation, which he fays the commons ought to fhew : but I flatter myfelf I have made it evident, that no member who fhould vote for an equal reprefentation, could be faid to " deftroy his immediate conftituent;" and nothing, to my mind, could be fo far from giving " an unlimited operation to the influence of the crown," as the making minifterial bribery in parliament, *impoffible.*

42. According to Junius's doctrine, I do not fee that the legiflature could, *de jure,* make *any* alteration in the prefent mode of electing reprefentatives: for, if the perfons and boroughs, now enjoying that *exclufive* power

power of choofing the houfe of commons, be juftly intitled to this exclufive power; and fhould have any part of it taken out of their hands, by " increafing the number of knights of fhires," cr by any other fimilar means, fuch a proceeding muft be a violation of their *exclufive* right; and muft, in a certain degree, " rob them of their freehold, their birth-right," This doctrine, therefore, overturns itfelf.

43. I am truly forry that fo argumentative and eloquent a writer fhould have formed, what appears to me, an erroneous opinion, on a point of fo much importance: nor do I think myfelf fortunate, in being obliged to take the contrary fide of an argument which he has once handled. Neverthelefs, having a full conviction of being on the fide of truth, and knowing that I am writing, not fpeaking, to the public, I have ventured to oppofe plain homely reafoning to all the powers of argument and eloquence, My principles I truft, are perfectly conftitutional. I may therefore leave them to their unaffifted operation on the good fenfe and fpirit of my countrymen.

44. I know, full well, how much the vicious part of every community affect to treat plans of reformation as chimerical,—as romantic, and utterly impracticable. And I know, too, that the reforming of our parliamentary jurifprudence hath been particularly fcoffed at, as the vifionary fcheme of refining fyftem-

fyftem-makers and ignorant enthufiafts. It
is not difficult to account for thefe infolences.
The vultures will hover, and flap, and fcream,
about the putrid carcafs on which they feed.
The Cornifh barbarians, notwithftanding Mr.
Burke's late humane act, will caft a longing
eye upon a wreck, and perfift in calling their
diabolical plunder a *right*, a *prefcriptive* right
of many ages. But I regard not the clamours
of the harpies; and I defpife their nonfenfe,
as fincerely as I abhor their principles.

45. The reader, if he will have the patience
to perufe a few dry pages of propofed regulations, fhall be convinced, that to elect an
annual parliament, and to eftablifh an equal
reprefentation, are things the moft fimple
and eafy in nature. If he ever thought
otherwife, he will be furprized that he could
have over-looked what will now appear to him
fo obvious. He muft have patience, I fay,
with this part of our work; except he can
delight in utility for its own fake alone. No
man looks for entertainment into an act of
parliament, or a body of civil regulations.
Sufficient, if they inform; and better clear
than elegant. For the fake of perfpicuity,
and in order to ftop the mouth of difingenuous
cavil, I muft defcend to fome minutiæ. He
who attacks national eftablifhments, fanctified
by time and cuftom, and interwoven with
the *felfifh interefts* of the moft powerful men
in the community; had need, even in the
moft

moſt enlightened and liberal age, to move
with circumſpection; and to omit nothing,
however trivial, which may ſerve to ſecure
the ground he gains, ſtep by ſtep, in making
his approaches. After all, we cannot alas!
do more than *prove* our propoſitions; and lay
down a plan for the undertaking in *theory*.
My fellow citizens muſt aſſiſt in carrying it
into *practice*. And to the few advocates for
their rights and liberties in parliament, it belongs to take the lead. Should *our* proof be
clearly made out, it will afford thoſe gentlemen the beſt of all opportunities of *proving*
their public integrity *beyond a doubt*. This,
I ſurely need not tell them, is the only thing
wanting, towards obtaining them the entire
confidence and ſupport of the people, in
effecting this, or any other neceſſary reformation in our government.

46. The whole iſland ſends to parliament
558 members. Of which number Scotland
ſends 45; England and Wales jointly, the
remaining 513. Let us, then, divide the ſaid
513 amongſt the counties of England and
Wales, in exact proportion to the reſpective
number of males in each county, who ſhall
be of a proper age to vote for repreſentatives
in parliament. I ſhould propoſe the age of
18 years, for two reaſons. 1. Becauſe, at
that age, a man is liable to ſerve himſelf, as a
military *repreſentative* of his country, in the
militia. And thus, the ſame pariſh rolls (of
which

which more hereafter) will shew at once, who are of an age to be *military* reprefentatives and *civil* electors. 2. Becaufe, I think at that age, a man is a fufficient judge between palpable right and wrong; and every way capable of nominating for himfelf a proper reprefentative: and the law of England thinks fo too, for " at twelve years old, he may take " the oath of allegiance; at 14, is at years of " difcretion, and therefore may confent or " difagree to marriage, and *may choofe his* " *guardian* a." To the end of making this proportional divifion, throughout the kingdom, nothing is neceffary but correct county rolls, taken from the refpective roll of each parifh in every county. In like manner, let the 45 Scotch members be proportionably divided amongft the counties of Scotland: and in other refpects let their elections be regulated by the fame rules as are hereafter laid down for England and Wales.

N. B. The feveral counties, for all times to come, might continue to fend up to parliament the fame number of members, as fhould appear to be their proportion on this *firft* enrolment of their men competent to vote in elections; notwithftanding any future alteration in their refpective numbers. No alteration, in point of numbers, could poffibly be fo confiderable, as ever to give them either

a Blackf. Comm. vol. I. p. 463.

caufe

caufe or inclination to demand a new proportional divifion of the members to be made throughout the kingdom.

47. The city of London might be confidered as a county to all intents and purpofes; having, in matters of election, no connexion whatever with the reft of Middlefex.

48. Every other city and town might be allowed, out of the number of members returnable by the whole county of which it made a part, to elect its own proportion feparately; and all the reft fhould be chofen at the county election. But all fractions in the number of competent men, proportioned to one reprefentative, to be in favour of the county. Eftimating the whole number of fouls at 6,000,000; the competent men will be 1,500,000; and the number of thofe anfwering to one reprefentative will be 2924. A town containing that number would be intitle to fend one member; twice that number, or 5848, two members; and fo on. But if it fhould enrol only 5800, the fraction fhould be in favour of the county, and the town fend up but one member. In like manner, if it enrolled but 2923, it fhould not elect feparately, but jointly with the county.

N. B. While no fmaller number than 2924 competent inhabitants could poffibly have the election of a reprefentative to themfelves, I fhould hope *Harrington's* and *Burgh's* propofed rule for ' an exclufion by rotation' of

the

the members of the houfe of commons would
be found wholly unneceffary; at leaft I would
have it by all means confined to the reprefentatives of cities and towns. There can be no
fuppofing that county elections, *fuch as I pro-*
pofe, could be influenced by any man or men
however great: and without very fufficient
caufe, the commons fhould not be deprived
of their right to elect any men, and efpecially
thofe of whofe integrity and abilities they had
had proof. Nor, in my opinion, fhould men
of worth, who had a laudable ambition of
being diftinguifhed for public fervices, have
any unneceffary obftacles thrown in their
way. ' A rotation, it is true, might give all
' perfons of confequence their turns in the
' government;' and to this Mr. *Burgh* feems
to think gentlemen of property have a *right*.
But the idea of fuch a right is totally inconfiftent with the inherent right of the
commons to have thofe for reprefentatives
whom they prefer to all others. Such an
idea of *right*, on the part of gentlemen,
would tend alfo to abate their *emulation*; and
confequently they would become lefs anxious
to merit the diftinction, by a due application
to the ftudy of public affairs, and by the
practice of private virtues; which, *then* would
be ftronger recommendations to the people's
favour, than a nabob's fortune or a minifter's
letter. I own that too much attention cannot
be given to *Burgh's* argument in favour of

a roa rotation; which is, the certainty with which it would operate in exterminating corrup-tion; and therefore, rather than have an ap-prehenfion of that kind, it would doubtlefs be better to have no feparate town or city elections at all, but for the counties, by their parifhes, to choofe the whole number of members collectively. By the feparate elec-tions, I only meant to provide more effectually for the particular patronage of the capital trading and manufacturing towns.

49. Any city or town fhould, on the fame principle, either attain or lofe its privilege of electing feparately, by an increafe or dimi-nution of its inhabitants.

N. B. Thefe queftions, as matters now ftand, muft be tried by the Houfe of Com-mons themfelves, as they claim the right and exercife the power of being the only judges of their own privileges. But perhaps it might, neverthelefs, be an improvement, and no way injurious to their privileges, to erect a new Court of Record for the trying of them, as well as thofe of the Houfe of Lords: the judges to be on the fame foot as in the other courts, their jurifdiction marked out, and the forms of trial fettled. The king himfelf is not the fole judge of his own privileges and prerogative: why then fhould either of the inferior branches of the legiflature have fuch a power? A court of parliamentary privileges might prevent the wafte of much precious

time

time loft to legiflation ; and its proceedings would probably be more efficient than thofe of election committees.

50. In every parifh, throughout each county, there fhould be kept, by proper parifh officers, under the checque of the minifter, a correct roll of the names of all the competent men within the fame. This roll fhould be compleated afrefh before the 1ft day of May in every year, taking in the names of all thofe perfons who might arrive at the age of competency on or before the 1ft day of June.

51. From thefe rolls, the Sheriff of the county, (to whom copies of them fhould be immediately tranfmitted) fhould make out a county roll; correcting it and compleating it annually before the 1ft day of June.

52. The whole Houfe of Commons fhould be chofen on the 1ft day of June in every year, except it fell on a Saturday or a Sunday. In either of thofe cafes, on the Monday next after.

53. Both in county, and town elections, the commons fhould all vote by *parifhes*; and the elections fhould in all places begin in the morning, between 6 and 8 o'clock. The minifter (if one in the parifh) affifted by the other parifh officers to take the poll, and to make his report of the fame, figned by himfelf and his affiftants, to the fheriff.

N. B.

N. B. This regulation would keep the people all peaceably at their own homes, fave them expences, and prevent the fhocking debaucheries fo common at our prefent elections. It would alfo put a fure period to all riots and diforderly proceedings: becaufe the fuccefs of a riotous party in one parifh, would contribute little or nothing to the general fuccefs of the candidate they fhould efpoufe. But thefe effects are all obvious.—

54. The parifh reports fhould, by the refpective conftables, be all delivered to the Sheriff of the County, affifted by a Bench of Juftices of the Peace (not fewer than five) on fuch day, and at fuch place, within the county, as the fheriff fhould appoint, not being later than the laft day of June[e]. The conftable to atteft upon oath, if required, the figning of the minifter and other parifh officers; which, for that reafon fhould be done in his prefence.

55. From the whole collection of parifh reports the Sheriff, affifted as aforefaid, fhould make out his general county report: not only diftinguifhing thofe candidates who appeared to be duly elected members of the parliament; but fetting down alfo the name of every other,

[e] The three ridings of Yorfhire might elect their members feparately; and other large counties might be fubdivided. The fenior juftice on the bench might, in thofe cafes, officiate for the Sheriff, where he could not be prefent in perfon.

and

and over againſt them reſpectively, the number of lawful ſuffrages in favour of each.

56. In all cities and towns, the chief magiſtrate to officiate as ſheriff, and be properly
aſſiſted by inferior magiſtrates.

57. All the general reports ſhould be
tranſmitted by the ſeveral Sheriffs and chief
magiſtrates, to the clerk of the crown, on or
before the 14th day of July.

58. Every candidate ſhould be obliged to
ſignify in writing, to the Sheriff or chief
magiſtrate of the county or place to which he
offered his ſervices, ſuch his intention and
offer, after a preſcribed form, and never
later than the 1ſt day of May, being a month
before the election. At the ſame time he
ſhould tranſmit an affidavit of his qualification,
after a preſcribed form alſo. For a county
member the qualification ſhould be a landed
eſtate; and 400l. *per ann.* might be ſufficient:
for London it might be the ſame; or a property in the kingdom of 12000l.; for other
cities and towns 300l. *per ann.* in land, or
9000l. in other property; clear of all debts
and demands.

59. The names of all theſe candidates
ſhould be immediately publiſhed by the ſeveral ſheriffs and chief magiſtrates throughout
their diſtricts; and a liſt of them alſo ſhould
be delivered to the conſtable of every pariſh,
on or before the 20th day of May.

60. It

60. It ſhould be made unlawful for any poll to be taken otherwiſe than by ballot. This would prevent undue influence, perſonal offence, and ſelf reproach. But it would not prevent that influence which ought to follow worth, wiſdom and a right uſe of wealth. Gentlemen ſo diſtinguiſhed, would always be ſure of being elected when they ſhould offer themſelves; and their recommendations of others would alſo have due weight. A ſeat in the houſe of commons would then be an honour: and an honour not to be obtained for merit at Newmarket, the gaming table, or in a cotillon. The following mode of balloting, being very ſimple, might anſwer the purpoſe. Before the miniſter and other pariſh officers taking the poll, place three jars or other veſſels, one of them being *white*, one *red* and one *black*; and give to every voter, the names of all the candidates, each on a ſeparate paper. Let the voter put in the *white* veſſel as many of theſe candidates names, as there are repreſentatives to be choſen; and into the *red* veſſel let him put the names of the remaining candidates. But if there ſhould be any one or more candidates for whom he ſhould not chooſe to give any favourable vote at all, he ſhould put their names into the *black* veſſel. Let the names depoſited within the *white* and *red* veſſels be made into two ſeparate liſts; with the number of the ſuffrages for each candidate

'didate over againſt his name: and let both
the liſts be audibly and diſtinctly read over to
all the people preſent. The names in the
black veſſel ſhould be burnt, in the preſence of
the people, unopened.

61. The ſeveral Sheriffs and chief magiſtrates ſhould alſo make their general reports of the non-elected candidates, as well
as of the members choſen; together with
the number of ſuffrages in favour of each.

62. Let there be no re-elections within the
year: but, in caſe of a member's dying or
vacating his ſeat in the houſe, let the ſpeaker
ſummon to parliament in his ſtead, him,
amongſt the non-elected candidates for the
ſame county or town, who ſhall have the
greateſt number of ſuffrages in his favour.
But, in caſe of that liſt being exhauſted, and
a vacancy in the houſe ſtill remaining, leave
it unfilled till the next election.

N. B. Should this happen, though it is
not likely, the ſhortneſs of the parliament
will prevent any ill conſequences enſuing.
The electors will ſtill have ſeveral repreſentatives in the houſe. Beſides, in ſuch a parliament as we here propoſe, there will be a
different kind of attendance on their duty from
what we now experience, and we may be
certain that neither the common buſineſs nor
eſſential intereſts of their conſtituents will be
neglected, on account of the abſence of a few
members.

N   63. Pro-

63. Provided there fhould ever be a de-
ficiency of candidates by the time prefcribed,
viz. 1ft May; for giving any county or town
its proportion of members, and providing alfo
for the fucceffions mentioned in the foregoing
article, to the amount of *one* non-elected candidate to every *three* members, I would propofe to remedy that defect thus:—Let every
voter be allowed to give in as many additional
names of his own choofing as may be wanting,
and put them into the *white* or the *red* veffel,
as he fhould prefer one to the other in his own
mind [f]. But it fhould be neceffary that
thefe *involuntary* candidates (if I may ufe that
liberty of expreffion) fhould refide within the
county or town of the *electors*, and be qualified for the reprefentation; or elfe their nomination to be fet afide by the fheriff and his
affiftant magiftrates. Such involuntary perfons, being either originally elected members,
or called up afterwards to fill a vacancy, fhould
be obliged to do parliamentary duty, on condition of being paid two guineas *per diem* during
parliamentary attendance, and one fhilling a
mile travelling expences by their conftitu-

[f] As, in fuch a cafe, the people of different parifhes
throughout a county would doubtlefs nominate a confiderable variety of gentlemen, this provifion would
effectually fecure both the requifite number of members,
and amply provide a fucceffion, ready to fill fuch vacancies
as might happen within the year.

ents;

ents; the fame to be raifed by a rate for that purpofe [s].

N. B. Practifing phyficians, furgeons, apo-thecaries, and attorneys at law; fhop-keepers, and fick perfons fhould be exempted.

64. Whenever the numbers of the fuffrages in any election fhould be equal, the decifion fhould be made by lot; the juftices preparing, and the fheriff drawing, the fame.

65. Every man being intitled to vote fomewhere, none fhould vote in more places than one: (See § 17) nor fhould any one in-rol himfelf in a new place, without producing a certificate, in due form, of his name having been erafed from the former roll.

66. For the cities of London and Weft-minfter and for the borough of Southwark, no man ought to be competent to vote or to be inrolled as a voting inhabitant, who had a home, or occupied any houfe or lodging what-foever in the country; excepting merchants, dealers and chapmen, and fhop-keepers.

N. B. Thefe places conftantly overflow with people who are from their own homes and parifhes. It is therefore fit fome reftraint of this kind fhould be practifed. Not, how-ever, that any breach of this rule could ever

[s] They would be all known to the Sheriff, though their names fhould not be fent to him on a feparate lift : becaufe of their not having been in his own original lift of candidates fent to the parifhes before the election.

be

be of any ill confequence; fo long as all the elections throughout the kingdom were carrying on at the fame inftant.

67. In London, and all other populous cities or towns, the parifhes, if too large, fhould be fo fubdivided, as to have the elections always over in one day.

68. Let it be made part of the very conftitution of parliament always to meet without any fummons at Weftminfter (except the king in a cafe of neceffity fhould appoint any other place) upon *a fixed day* within one certain week of November, provided his majefty had not affembled them fooner; and again, upon *one fixed day* in January; and to fit each time for *a certain limited term*, and fo much longer, as his majefty fhould have occafion for their attendance: not, however, later than till the 20th day of May.

N. B. In order to the fecuring of thefe points, every form and engagement the moft facred that could be devifed fhould be made ufe of by the refpective parties. In the firft place, every candidate fhould, together with the affidavit of his qualification, (§ 58) tranfmit alfo (and every time he became a candidate) to the fheriff, another oath; in which he fhould have fworn that, provided he fhould become a member of parliament in confequence of the enfuing election, he neither would fit nor act himfelf as a member of the fame, nor give his confent for any other

fo

fo to do, longer than the 20th day of May
next following. Secondly, it fhould be an
indifpenfible requifite, in order to conftitute
a legal election, that he who prefided at the
poll fhould make proclamation, that ' the
' competent men then and there affembled
' were to proceed to give their votes towards
' an election of fit perfons to reprefent them-
' felves and all the competent men in the
' county (or otherwife as the cafe might be)
' to which they belonged, in a parliament
' which was to *ceafe, determine* and *expire* on
' the 20th day of May next following.' And
an atteftation of this proclamation having been
made fhould be part of the conftable's oath
(§ 54) before the fheriff and his affiftant magiftrates; and in their general report of the
election, the term for which the reprefentatives were chofen fhould be particularly fpe-
cified. I call it *report*, and not *return*, becaufe then, the parliament would not be
chofen in confequence of the *king's writs to the
fheriffs*, &c. but in confequence of the general
law and conftitution of parliaments, arifing
from the right of the commons fpontaneoufly
to appoint, and fend up, their reprefentatives
" twice in the year, or oftener, if need fhould
" be, to treat of the government of God's
" people; how they fhould keep themfelves
" from fin, fhould live in quiet, and fhould
" receive right;" according to that " which
" was ordained" by *Alfred* the beft of all
our

our kings except his prefent majefty "for a per-
" petual ufage." Nor would it, in my opinion,
be too much were the king required, not
only at his coronation, but annually, on the
firft day of meeting his parliament, and before
he entered the houfe of lords, to take an oath,
in prefence of fome of the members of the
lower houfe, that he never would attempt to
prevent the appointed fittings of parliament,
nor give his affent to any law for prolonging
either the then prefent, or any other future,
parliament beyond its proper and limited
term of a year wanting eleven days. But,
to return ;

69. Let all parifh rolls be truly and carefully kept, on pain of fome confiderable pe-
nalty. The names to be regularly numbered,
and no alteration to be made of their nu-
merical order, on account of names legally
erafed, until the expiration of feven years.
At the commencement of every eighth year, a
new roll to be made out; omitting the erafed
names on the former roll, and numbering the
new roll as at firft. The general county roll
to be renewed and frefhly numbered in like
manner, and at the fame time.

70. All rolls fhould be kept on paper of
a fixed fize, printed in a form prefcribed by
law. And the fame fhould be regulated with
regard to the paper to be made ufe of at elections, for fetting down the names of the
candidates.

71. All

71. All place men and all military men (except of the militia) as being reprefentatives of, and fubject to influence from, the *crown*, fhould be totally ineligible to fit as reprefentatives of the *commons*: but a certain number from the civil department, as well as from the army and navy, fhould be intitled to a place in the houfe, and allowed the fame freedom of fpeech as the members; though by no means permitted to vote.

No penfioner of the crown (except fuch as had obtained their penfions for life, and to whom they were given with the exprefs confent or approbation of a houfe of commons;) no perfon enjoying any eleemofynary ftipend at the will of another, (a very near relation excepted) fhould be eligible. Nor any clergyman in holy orders; nor Irifh peers; they both having duties elfewhere which they ought not to neglect. Quitting fuch duties, is no recommendation of them to the important truft of being our legiflators. Nor, perhaps, would it be improper to exclude the heirs apparent to peerages: but of that, I am not fixed in my opinion.

72. Thus, then, have I done my beft to fketch out a new parliamentary plan: let others alter it at their pleafure; provided only that they *mend it*. Where, now, is the impracticability of making our reprefentation *equal*; where the difficulty, the expence, or trouble of *annual* elections! For my own part
I think

I think none but old women can suppofe them; and none but men of very bad principles and the very worft defigns, can ftill urge their exiftence. I am fure that a village conftable would be afhamed to acknowledge himfelf incapable of conducting the whole of it: and I know that the laws by which we now raife our militia, are attended with more difficulties and more trouble ten times over. But that the execution of fuch a plan will be oppofed by the court and its tools, I likewife have no doubt. And I can eafily forefee, that, for want of an honeft and *direct* objection to it, they will indirectly attack it, by an artful vindication, as they will pretend, of the royal prerogative, upon which, according to their doctrines, it incroaches. I think it, therefore, neceffary, before I difmifs the fubject, to fpeak a little to that point.

73. As I wifh to give every *honeft* doubter all reafonable fatisfaction, at the fame time that I would fhew a proper attention to all that the court can object to my propofed abridgment of the prerogative, I will begin with taking Judge Blackftone's opinion on the point in queftion. " As to the manner and " time of affembling;" fays he, " the par-" liament is regularly to be fummoned by the " king's writ or letter, iffued out of chancery " by advice of the privy council, at leaft forty " days before it begins to fit. It is a branch " of the royal prerogative that no parliament " can

" can be convened by its own authority, or
" by the authority of any, except the king
" alone. And this prerogative *is founded upon*
" *very good reafon.* For, fuppofing it had
" a right to meet fpontaneoufly, without
" being called together, it is impoffible to
" conceive that all the members, and each of
" the houfes, would agree unanimoufly upon
" the proper time and place of meeting: and
" if half of the members met, and half
" abfented themfelves, who fhall determine
" which is really the legiflative body, the part
" affembled, or that which ftays away? It
" is therefore neceffary that the parliament
" fhould be called together at a determinate
" time and place: and highly becoming its
" dignity and independence, that it fhould
" be called together by none but one of
" its own conftituent parts: and, of the three
" conftituent parts, this office can only ap-
" pertain to the king: as he is a fingle perfon,
" whofe will may be uniform and fteady; the
" firft perfon in the nation, being fuperior to
" both houfes in dignity; and the only branch
" of the legiflature that has a feparate ex-
" iftence, and is capable of performing any
" act at a time when no parliament is in
" being." But what does all this amount to,
which can any way fhew the impropriety of
the parliament's meeting at " a determinate
time and place" previoufly agreed on, by *all*

O   the

the branches of the legiflature? If " it be
" highly becoming its dignity and inde-
" pendence, that it fhould be called to-
" gether by none but *one* of its confti-
" tuent parts," furely its dignity will be
ftill better provided for, when it fhall
come together by the unanimous agreement
of all the *three*. So much of the prerogative
as can be of *any ufe*, will ftill be left to the
crown, fhould the regulation I propofe become part of the conftitution of parliament:
the king may ftill fummon his parliament, at
any time *before* its appointed meeting; he
may keep it affembled *beyond the fixed period*
for its fitting; and, after its difmiffion, *he
may call it again*, if occafion require, and
keep it in attendance the full period of its
exiftence.

74. Let any man but confider our very
multifarious national bufinefs, and reflect upon
the prodigious number of bills which are
paffed in every feffion of parliament; and then
fay, whether or not fome *certain* parliamentary attendance be not abfolutely neceffary.
Let him alfo confider of what utility and
convenience it would be to the public, always
to know the times of its meetings; in order
that all perfons, being interefted in any bills
which were to come before the houfes,
might prepare themfelves accordingly: let
him, moreover, call to mind that, as kings
have

have heretofore governed *without* parliaments for a long time, they may poffibly attempt to do fo again, if we do not take care to prevent them; and I think he will hold it ridiculous, to talk of its being a prerogative of the king, to have the fittings of parliaments *entirely* at his mercy. Prerogative is "a power of doing public good *without* a rule." This evidently implies that its *only* fphere of action, is in thofe cafes alone, where the law *cannot* provide a proper rule; for, to fuppofe that prerogative could in any cafe be allowed, where fuch a rule *could* be provided, would be to' admit that prerogative is as good as law. This, however, is no doctrine of the Englifh conftitution. The *aula regia*, erected by *William the conqueror*, followed the king's perfon in all his progreffes and expeditions[h]; and *confequently*, fat at *his pleafure*; till *magna charta* removed the grievance, by confining it to a *determinate place*, in Weftminfter Hall; where of courfe it became not only a ftationary, but a *regular* judicature. And we are informed that it was through "fear of the 'annual parliaments" of thofe days, that this *aula regia* was erected in the royal palace, and vefted with a portion of that power which, till then, the *wittena gemote*, or parliament,

[h] Blackftone's Com. vol. 3, p. 38.

had

had been poffeffed of. It muft be in the nature of every tyrant, however fuccefsful, to dread an annual parliament truly reprefenting the whole body of commons: while, on the other hand, fuch a council will always be moft acceptable, to a prince of genuine virtue and magnanimity; who, like his prefent majefty, wifhes to be the father of a free people; and therefore will rather defire to know their *real fentiments* and *interefts*, than to be deceived by the lying flatteries and mifreprefentations of fycophants and public robbers. Conceiving, as I do, that fome of the meetings of parliament ought to be regular and certain, and by no means to depend on the will of the king; it is natural that I fhould deny it to be the prerogative of the crown, to *diffolve* a parliament, meaning only an *annual* parliament, before it fhould have fat a fufficient time for ordering the public affairs. We very well know how the power of *diffolving* has heretofore been practifed. If the king is to have a power to *prevent* a parliament from affembling; and likewife, when affembled, a power to *diffolve* it again; is not this fufficient for rendering a parliament a mere cypher in government? A power that fhould *never* be made ufe of, *ought not to exift.* No matter, as to the probabilities of fuch an abufe. But we know that it is *poffible;* becaufe it *has* happened. The commons have

a *right*

a *right* to confult with the other two branches
of the legiflature, every year, or oftner, if
need be, on public affairs; and they have a
right alfo to counfel the king on all matters
of ftate; to enquire into abufes, and to call
minifters to account: hence, it ought not to
be in the power of the fovereign to prevent
them. For them to have a *right* to do all
thefe things; and for him to have *a power to
deprive* them of the means of exercifing this
right, is a contradiction.—But the very
idea of a power in the crown to diffolve
at pleafure an *annual* parliament, is particularly irreconcileable with reafon[1]. By its
negative, it can effectually prevent any houfe
of commons from doing any legiflative injury
to the conftitution, fhould it at any time ma-
nifeft fuch a difpofition; and the commons
at large, to *whom alone* it belongs to *difmifs their
own fervants*, would very foon have an opportunity of difcarding them, and appointing
more trufty ones in their room. So, though
in the judge's opinion, the prerogative of
convening the parliament at the pleafure of
the king, be " founded upon *very good*

---

[1] One abufe begets another. While under the im-
pofition of long parliaments, we feel fome confolation in
vefting the crown with the power of diffolution. But
what a wretched condition are the commons in, when
they have no way of getting rid of fervants who wrong
and infult them, but by petitioning the crown !

reafons;"

reasons;" there are still *much better* reasons to be given, why it ought to have its *fixed*, as well as its *precarious*, sittings.

75. The more we contemplate an annual parliament, and those other barriers of liberty I propose to have erected, the more I am persuaded we shall become attached to them. I am sorry to find Junius no friend to such parliaments. " Whenever," says he, " the " question of annual parliaments shall be " seriously agitated, I will endeavour (and if " I live will assuredly attempt it) to convince " the English nation, by arguments to my " understanding unanswerable, that they " ought to insist upon a triennial, and banish " the idea of an annual parliament." I have been often, and much at a loss, to discover what could have been his reasons for this declaration. The more I have myself contemplated the subject, and drawn comparisons between parliaments of different durations, the more confirmed have I always been in giving the preference to an annual one, provided *it were properly chosen*. Indeed I never could arrive at any other satisfactory conclusion; but here my mind rests in security, and I find every satisfaction which the case requires or admits of. I hope the able writer abovementioned is still alive, and will no longer delay to favour the public with his sentiments at large on this great question.

If

If it it be not full time that it were " ferioufly
" agitated," I have formed a wrong opinion;
having very ferioufly difcuffed it to the beft
of my poor abilities. Satisfied as I am at
prefent of the wifdom of recurring to annual
parliament, I fhall very readily change that
fentiment in favour of triennial, or even feptennial ones, provided any one will convince
me by unanfwerable arguments that either of
them are entitled to a preference. After all
our differences in opinion, 'tis truth alone
that can do us effential fervice. He who has
any other controverfial purfuit, which caufes
him wilfully to deviate from that, is, in
my eftimation, a peft to fociety. Should I
prefume to guefs at the objections of Junius
to annual parliaments, I fhould fuppofe they
probably arofe from his previous ideas concerning the impracticability of reftoring an
equal reprefentation. On that point, perhaps, the reader now agrees with me in think-
ing, that he had formed but a defective judg-
ment. His error, in that particular, I conceive to be full fufficient for giving birth to
others of no fmall moment, with regard to
the moft eligible length of parliaments.
Were, indeed, no other alteration to be
made in our reprefentation, than that which
he fpeaks of with approbation, of " increafing
" the number of knights of fhires;" I confefs that an annual parliament, fuch as we
fhould

ſhould then have, and ſo choſen as it would
ſtill be, would be little better than the preſent. Probably not at all: pſſiobly it might
make things worſe. Such a parliament, being
ſtill within the reach of corruption, would
doubtleſs be corrupted. A very large proportion would ſtill be *founded* upon corruption: the rotten boroughs would ſtill contaminate the houſe of commons. Without a
much deeper reformation, there would continue to be juſt as many ſaleable ſeats to diſ-
poſe of in ſuch a parliament, as in any former
one. They would moſt likely, in ſuch a caſe,
be contracted for by a kind of conditional
leaſe, for three, five, ſeven or more ſucceſſive
years, at a ſtipulated annual rent, according
to the inclinations or views of the leſſees. The
borough brokers and maſters of calculation
would ſoon fix their market price for every
ſuppoſeable term of years. Should it be in
the power of a majority, or even of a conſiderable number of the members, thus to ſecure
their places in parliament for any propoſed
time, what would it avail the nation that it
were *called* an annual parliament? In order
to render ſo great a portion of corruption of
no effect in the houſe, the knights of ſhires
muſt be increaſed to a number that would
preclude all poſſibility of ſober counſel and
debate. But in what conceivable aſſembly
would it be poſſible to admit ſuch a degree
of

of corruption, without a certainty of its producing very ill effects! An annual parliament without an equal reprefentation would be of no ufe; as, on the other hand, an equal reprefentation without an annual parliament would afford us no fecurity. Together, they would form a palladium of liberty. Venality would be banifhed, and tyranny bound. Why, in God's name, fhould we fuffer any known and palpable corruption to contaminate the fource of legiflation!

76. I only agree with a very great number of the beft and wifeft men of the age, when I fay that except parliamentary proftitution be done clean away, the liberties of this country have not long to exift. I have endeavoured to do the duty of a citizen, by attempting to point out the ready means of effecting this great purpofe. My fellow citizens muft judge how far I have fucceeded; and determine for themfelves whether they will neglect them and fink into flavery, or adopt them and be free. May that Being who gave us our freedom infpire us with a due fenfe of fo tranfcendent a bleffing, and enable us to tranfmit it unimpaired to our pofterity!

P   CON-

CONCLUSION.

I CANNOT but feel the ftrongeft per-
fuafion that the *facility* of annually electing
our lower houfe of parliament, and of reftoring a full, equal and perfect reprefentation
to the commons, is in the foregoing pages de-
monftrated: and I hope my reader agrees with
me, in the idea of its being abfolutely neceffary
to make thefe reforms immediately. Now it
only remains to infpire him with a confidence
that they may be effected, even againft the
whole force and fraud of minifterial oppofition; and to adjure him, as he fhall anfwer
it hereafter, not to be wanting to his country
on this great occafion: but to do his duty to
that, I had almoft faid divine conftitution,
under which he lives, and under which he
looks for peace and protection. No man can
plead impotency without confeffing difincli-
nation. The pooreft peafant of our ftate, I
have fhewn to be an important member of it;
and that he hath as high a title to liberty as
the moft illuftrious nobleman. I have fhewn
likewife that, in juftice, the voice of the
peafant goes as far as that of the richeft com-
moner towards the nomination of a member of
a parliament. The name of a peafant will confequently, be of as much value in a petition to
the

the throne, or any public act of the commons in their focial capacity, as that of any
freeholder or borough voter whatever. It
will be the fignature of a freeman : of a man
every way intitled to the protection of the laws,
and competent to a fhare in the framing of
them. To vindicate this right is doubtlefs of
the laft importance ; for liberty, like learn-
ing, is beft preferved by its being widely dif-
fufed through fociety. *Numbers* are its
health, ftrength and life. But, to return, let my
reader, if he have a wifh for reformation, either
recollect or read what is propofed in the con-
clufion of the political difquifitions, concerning a grand national affociation
for reftoring the conftitution.
It would be impertinent to repeat what is
there written. I will only endeavour to throw
in my fmall contribution towards removing
the difficulties of carrying fuch a noble fcheme
into practice. As foon as leaders worthy of
fuch a caufe fhall have made themfelves known
to the public (and fuch I have reafon to believe will foon appear) it may be prefumed
that they will be provided with a concife and
clear ftate, of the evils flowing from long
parliaments; of the injuftice and abfurdity of
fuch parliaments themfelves; of the infinite
advantages from their removal; and of the
method propofed for this falutary work.
They will doubtlefs lay a reprefentation of

their

thefe matters before the king himfelf, and
fhew him how fatally he has been mifadvifed
by his minifters. If his majefty's wifdom
be in any degree proportioned to his known
goodnefs of heart, he will be awakened
as from a dream, and all will go well. He
can at his pleafure make any parliaments annual by diffolutions; and, patronized by him,
the whole plan for repairing the foundation
and the fortifications of liberty will be exe-
cuted with infinitely lefs trouble than it coft
to pafs the act for eftablifhing popery in a
Britifh province, or to enact any one of thofe
laws by which we weakly attempted to en-
flave the colonies. Such an act of wifdom
and goodnefs would place the name of *George
the Third* the foremoft on the roll of patriot
kings : and the gratitude of his people would
give him every thing in return fhort of ado-
ration. He would then be great and powerfull
indeed! But, fhould it be the misfortune of
this country, that its fovereign fhould have
been fo effectually blinded to the only caufes
from which national profperity, regal dignity
and fplendour can be derived; fhould the
royal mind be warped by prejudice and un-
alterably fixed in a preference to certain men
and their falfe principles of government;
and fhould ever fo exprefsly condemn
the propofed reformation; yet, it muft
not be defpaired of. If a king will not
be a father to his people, they muft take
care

care of themfelves. For the fake of more
formality, I will fuppofe our patriot leaders
to make their next attempt in the houfe
of commons. But we fhould be weak indeed
to expect any better fuccefs in that quarter.
Neverthelefs fuch a proceeding would be
highly proper: and it would be right to have
a compleat bill for the purpofe ready to lay
upon the table, *if permitted*. The *jocular*
Lord *North*, after once more diverting himfelf and his play-fellows with this ' popular
' fquib,' gives the ufual fignal, and, it is no
no no'd out of the houfe in an inftant, and
honour'd at its exit with a horfe laugh [k].
An immediate publication of it would however enable the people to judge, whether
fuch a bill or fuch a houfe were moft for
their fervice. And it would then be high
time that a national affociation were forthwith
fet on foot. But the principles upon which I
have proceeded in this effay direct, that it fhould
have a wider bafis than that propofed by the
author abovementioned. Inftead of being confined to ' men of property, and to be fubfcribed
by thofe only whofe names are in any tax-
book,' it muft take in *every* man who fhall
prefer liberty to flavery. A flight reflection
on the temper and difpofition of the times
will teach us, that it ought to be fo concerted
as not, by any means, to depend upon a

[k] Good God in heaven, how do fome men trifle with
the fate of this nation! Further Examination, p. 230.

coup

coup de main for its fuccefs: but fo, as to grow
into the approbation of the public more and
more, as it fhould be more and more examined
Its intrinfic worth ought to be fuch, that
it might at all times hereafter, though it
failed at firft, be appealed to as a model for a
perfect parliament. Time, and circumftances, and fufferings from mifgovernment,
would one day or other bring it into ufe: but
any great and fudden national calamity would
inftantly make all men come into it as into the
ark of their prefervation. Our fufferings, if
not our reafon, are likely enough to drive us
into it within a very fhort period of time;
but, fhould we even allow that every fervant
of the crown and every member of parliament were an undoubted patriot, yet we could
have no excufe whatever for delaying it; becaufe the meafure is right in itfelf, and a duty
we owe to pofterity; who might behold fe-
nators and courtiers of another caft. If we
be in earneft to ferve our country, we muft
have patience and perfeverance as well as zeal.
The patriot does not fay to himfelf, ' I will
labour in my country's caufe for two or three,
or for fix or feven years;' and then, if difap-
pointed, ' I will abandon it in vexation or defpair :' no—the love of his country he finds the
ruling paffion of his foul; and he knows that
the duties of patriotifm, the aggregate of all the
minor focial duties, cannot ceafe but with his
vital breath. It is to be hoped, therefore,
that

that amongft our leaders no unworthy ambition fhall mix with this facred bufinefs, no
rafhnefs dictate their counfels: but that
wifdom, magnanimity, and an unconquerable
fpirit of perfeverance fhall regulate and diftinguifh their whole conduct. Befides the
univerfality which feems to be effential to the
fcheme of an affociation, it muft be framed
with the utmoft fimplicity. The motives to
it fhould be fet forth as clearly and concifely
as poffible; the contraft between the evils to
be removed and the advantages to be gained
fhould be fhort and ftriking; the peafant
fhould be taught to know his own importance; that a majority of the people have at all
times a right to correct the government
at their own difcretion, fhould be incul-
cated and proved; and it fhould likewife
be fhewn, that a majority will always fuc-
ceed in any thing they fhall ferioufly and ftea-
dily attempt. A hand bill would be fufficient
for this purpofe. They fhould be circulated,
together with the forms of the affociation,
throughout every parifh, and in the greateft
abundance. And at the fame time draughts
of a petition to the throne, for his majefty's
concurrence and aid towards procuring the
object of the affociation, fhould likewife be
circulated for fubfcriptions. But yet there is
one meafure which, above all others,
would be neceffary towards the profpering of
our undertaking. The people muft be convinced

vinced that there is no trick in the bufinefs: that the leaders in it will not turn
out *Pulteneys* or *F——ds*. In order hereto,
it will be requifite, that thefe leaders fhould
jointly fubfcribe and publifh the moft explicit
declaration of their intentions; and the moft facred engagements that they will before all things
perfevere till death, both in and out of parliament, towards obtaining the great object of
the propofed affociation, a parliamentary
reformation. It were to be wifhed too they
would confine themfelves to this one article.
It includes all the reft. Without this, nothing elfe can be obtained; and if they could,
would not be worth contending for. But
let them not amufe us with general terms
and indefinite expreffions. Let them fay
what this reformation fhall be:—let them
tell it us exactly, in all its particulars.
Let us be thoroughly fatisfied that we are not
to be made the bubbles of their ambition;
and when we fhall have raifed them to the
high feats of power, that we fhall not find
our liberties in as low a condition as before.
    An affociation thus planned, thus patro-
nized, thus conducted, would unite all parties ; and foon take in almoft the whole of the
kingdom : — but why fhould I fay *almoft*, why
fhould I fuppofe any man bafe enough not to
be of it? Neither the farmer, nor the mechanic
                                        may

may perhaps know whether the Americans
are right or wrong in oppofing government;
but *every man* knows that an affembly of
honeft men is to be preferred to an affembly of
knaves. Hence we fhould foon fee the wide
difference between a party ftruggle, for petitions againft addreffes, and addreffes againft
petitions; and a national invitation to all men
of all parties to take care of their lives, liberties and properties. No man's party will
fuffer by an annual parliament; becaufe no
minifter of what party foever can have an
influence over it. By annual elections every
man will be at liberty to vote for gentlemen
of his own party once a year: and he will
then find, by the help of very little experience,
that men of fenfe, probity and religion,
notwithftanding fome immaterial differences
of fentiment, are all of one party in politics;
and will all agree in ferving their country,
and in keeping the power of kings and minifters within bounds. " A defigning mi-
" niftry defires no better than that the peo-
" ple's attention be engaged about trifling
" grievances, fuch as have employed us fince
" the late peace. This gives them an oppor-
" tunity of wreathing the yoke around our
" necks, becaufe it gives them a pretence for
" increafing the military force. Inftructing,
" petitioning, remonftrating, and the like,
" are good diverfion for a court; becaufe
" they know, that, in fuch ways, nothing
" will be done againft their power. A grand
" national affociation for obtaining an inde-
" pendent parliament would make them

Q   " tremble.

"tremble. For they know, that the nation,
" if in earneſt, would have it, and that
" with the ceſſation of their influence in par-
" liament, their power muſt end '." It will
perhaps be ſaid that ' the members of an
' aſſociation can only petition the throne;
' that 60,000 of the ſubjects petitioned in the
' year 1769 for a diſſolution of the then parlia-
' ment ᵐ, and were anſwered only by a royal
' nod, and that, no nod of approbation;
' whereupon the ſaid 60,000 perſons were
' obliged to put up quietly with the contempt
' they met with.' I anſwer, that an aſſociated
nation may do more than petition, or re-
monſtrate either. There is nothing it cannot do but what is naturally impoſſible. It
can level a throne with the earth, and tram-
ple authority in the duſt. And it can do theſe
things of *right*. Nothing but its own belief
of their expediency to do it ſervice, can
preſerve them from its deſtroying hand. But
this nation knows too well the excellency of

¹ Pol. Diſq. v. 3. p. 455.
ᵐ Ibid. ——— 1.——— 35. where you will likewiſe find
theſe words; " It was moved in the houſe of commons,
" that, in their addreſs, in anſwer to the above profound
" ſpeech" (the king's upon the horned cattle) " the houſe
" ſhould declare their intention of enquiring into the
" cauſes of the preſent diſcontents. Several of the courtly
" members gravely denied that there was any diſcontent
" in the kingdom, though they knew that 60000 had
" ſubſcribed petitions for diſſolution of parliament. They
" might have argued more plauſibly, that there was no
" parliament then exiſting. For it will appear preſently,
" that a tenth part of the above number ſends in the ma-
" jority of the houſe. And if the voluntary petition
" of 60,000 deſerves no regard, ſurely the bought votes
" of 5000 ought to go for nothing.

its

its conftitution of government, to think of
doing the fmalleft injury to any branch of it.
Affociated to a man, the throne, the peerage,
the houfe of reprefentatives would be fo far
from being in danger, that, to refcue them
from abufe, to repair them, to ftrengthen
them, to re-edify and adorn them, could be
its fole object.

That fuch an affociation may take place, if
need be, is my ardent prayer; and I hope
there lives not that man upon our ifle fo unworthy of the fociety of men, who, if need
were, would not fubfcribe it with his blood,

F I N I S.

LIST of NEW BOOKS, Printed for J. ALMON, in Piccadilly.

A LETTER from Governor Pownall to
Adam Smith, LLD, and FRS. Being
an Examination of feveral Points of Doctrine
laid down in his Inquiry into the Nature and
Caufes of the Wealth of Nations. 4to. 1s. 6d.

A Letter to the Rev. Jofiah Tucker, D. D.
Dean of Gloucefter, in Anfwer to his humble
Addrefs and Earneft Appeal, &c. With a
Poftfcript, in which the prefent War againft
America is fhewn to be the Effect, not of the
Caufes affigned by Him and Others, but of a
fixed Plan of Adminiftration, founded in
Syftem: The Landed oppofed to the Com-
mercial Intereft of the State, being as the
Means in order to the End. By Samuel Eft-
wick, LLD. Affiftant Agent for the Ifland of
Barbadoes. 1s. 6d.

The Letters of VALENS; with a Preface,
and Corrections, by the Author. 3s.

The Hiftory of New-York, from the firft
Difcovery. With a Defcription of the Country,
an Account of the Inhabitants, their Trade,
Religious and Political State, &c. by W.
Smith, A. M. 8vo. 5s. boards, 6s. bound.

The Parliamentary Regifter, con- £. s. d.
taining an Account of the moft
interefting Speeches and Motions,
accurate Copies of all material
Papers and Letters, important

Evidence, Petitions, Bills, Protefts, &c. &c. in both Houfes of
Parliament, during the Years
1774, 1775. and 1776. Five
Volumes, half bound, 1l. 10s.
6d. and bound —— 1 13 •
The Debates and Proceedings of
the Houfe of Commons from 1773
to 1774, being the two laft Sef-
fions of the late Parliament. In
Two Volumes. in boards,
10s. 6d. and bound, —— 0 12 0
[Thefe two Volumes are a Continuation of the
former Debates to the End of the laft Parliament. It is humbly requefted of thofe Gentlemen who have not compleated their Sets, to
give Orders to their Bookfellers, or the Pub-
lifher, for the fame, as there will be no more
detached Volumes to be had after the prefent
Impreffion is fold.]
The Debates of the Houfe of Commons, from 1746 to 1772. Seven
Volumes —— 2 2 0
The Protefts of the Houfe of Lords,
from the firft upon Record; with
St. Amand's fcarce Tract on the
Legiflative Power of England.
Two Volumes —— 0 13 6

Debates of the Parliament of Ireland, in the Years 1775 and 1776; with all the authentic Papers relating to the Revenue, List of Pensions, &c. &c. half bound, 3s. 6d. bound — . o 4. o

Debates of the House of Commons of Ireland, during the Years 1763 and 1764. Dedicated, by Permission, to the Earl of Chatham. Taken by Sir James Caldwell, Bart. Two Volumes — o 12 o

Protests of the Lords of Ireland, from the first upon Record — o . 3 . 6.

All these Parliamentary Books being printed in Octavo, complete Sets may be had, uniformly bound, gilt and lettered. — 6 6 6

The REMEMBRANCER; or, Impartial Repository of Public Events. Published Monthly, Price One Shilling each Number. This Work began in June 1775, with the Commencement of Hostilities at Lexington in New-England, and has been continued Monthly to the present Time; containing from Time to Time, the Accounts, as given by both Sides, of every Public Transaction; with the several Journals, Resolutions, Declarations, &c. preserving a great Number of useful Papers not any where else to be met with.

Seventeen Numbers have been published, which make three Volumes; to each Volume is a copious Index, the whole half bound and lettered, 18s. 6d.

Select Tracts on American Affairs, from the Beginning of the Year 1768 to the End of 1775. In four Volumes, Octavo, half bound and lettered, One Guinea.

Journal of the American Congress for 1775, 3s.

The INTERIOR Country of North-America, from Montreal to New-York, which is become the Theatre of War, between the King's Troops and the Americans, is faithfully and accurately delineated in Governor Pownall's Map of the Middle Provinces. In this Map, are the Rivers, Falls, Lakes, Islands, Creeks, Towns, Forts, Hills, &c. are to be found, with their respective Names; so that the Routs of the several Armies, their occasional Posts, &c. may be traced with the greatest Ease and Exactness. This Map, having been collated and examined with the Surveys now lying at the Board of Trade, may be depended upon for Authenticity. It is further rendered useful, by a curious and copious topographical Description of the Country. Price 10s. 6d.

An Asylum for Fugitives. Price One Shilling each Number. (Published every three Months) Three Numbers make a Volume. The first Volume is just finished, and may be had sewed 3s. or bound, 3s. 6d.

A Companion to the Royal Kalendar; being a complete List of all the Changes made in Administration, from the Accession of the present King, to the present Time; with the late and present Parliaments; all the Alterations occasionally made in both; the Right of Election in each Place; in whose Favour Contests have been decided; the Names of the Candidates, Number of Voters, &c. 1s.

The Royal Kalendar, published annually, Containing the authentic Lists of all the Public Offices, correct Lists of both Houses of Parliament, including all the New Creations, the last Alterations in every Department, &c. &c. Price 2s. bound in red; 2s. 6d. with an Almanack; 3s. with the Companion; and quite complete with Companion and Almanack, 3s. 6d.

The Arms, Supporters, Crests and Mottoes of the Peers, Peeresses and Sees of Great Britain and Ireland: with the Baronets of England; all continued to November 1776.

The new present State of Great-Britain. Containing an Account of the Government of Great-Britain; the Power, Prerogatives, and Revenues of the King; the Laws, Customs, and Privileges of Parliament; and the Power and Methods of Proceeding in the several Courts of Justice. A Description of the Capitals of England and Scotland, their Government, Courts of Justice, principal Buildings, Trading, and other Companies, Privileges and Commerce, &c. &c. New Edition. Price 5s. bound.

A Collection of all the Treaties of Peace, Commerce, and Alliance, between Great-Britain and other Powers, from the Revolution (in 1688) to the present Time. Two Volumes. 12s.

No Pains have been spared to make this Work complete. Whenever Treaties have been published by Authority, or laid before Parliament, these Copies only have been followed; and whenever no Translation by Authority has appeared, the Original is inserted, together with a Translation.

A Collection of interesting Political Tracts from 1764, to the End of 1773. Eight Volumes 2l. 2s.

A Collection of interesting Letters from the public Papers, particularly including those written on the several Changes of Administration, the Taxation of the Colonies, &c. from the Accession of the present King to the End of 1768. Two Volumes, 8vo. 10s. 6d.

*** It is an Observation in Kennet's Register, which Lord Somers has chosen for his Motto, to his Collection of Tracts, " That the Bent and Genius of the Age is best known in a free Country, by the Pamphlets and Papers which daily come out."

Nov. 4, 1776.